West Acad
Emeritu

MW01195626

JESSE H. CHOPER
Professor of Law and Dean Emeritus
University of California, Berkeley

LARRY D. KRAMER
President, William and Flora Hewlett Foundation

JAMES J. WHITE
Robert A. Sullivan Emeritus Professor of Law
University of Michigan

West Academic Publishing's Law School Advisory Board

Judicial
Clerkships

Tessa L. Dysart

Clinical Professor of Law
University of Arizona James E. Rogers College of Law

A SHORT & HAPPY GUIDE® SERIES

WEST
ACADEMIC
PUBLISHING

a short & happy guide series is a trademark registered in the U.S. Patent and Trademark Office.

© 2023 LEG, Inc. d/b/a West Academic
      860 Blue Gentian Road, Suite 350
      Eagan, MN 55121
      1-877-888-1330
Printed in the United States of America

ISBN: 978-1-68561-062-3

To Mom & Dad for believing in my wildest dreams.

Acknowledgments

This might be the most difficult section of a book to write. Inevitably, once I start listing people, I am sure to inadvertently forget someone. Nonetheless, here we go!

First, I owe a debt of gratitude to Judge Dennis W. Shedd, whom I clerked for many years ago. I learned so much about the law (and college football) from Judge Shedd. My time working in his chambers was certainly a highlight of my career. Thanks also to Tony Emmanuel, Judge Shedd's career clerk, and the other chambers team—Jeff, Fraser, and Kathy. I also learned much from you, and we shared many a good meal together.

To my many friends who clerked or are currently on the bench. Thank you for answering my social media questions about clerking. Several of your comments have made their way into this book. A special thanks to Laura Ellingson, Leah Tedford, and Andrew Kartchner for reading chapters and providing feedback. I appreciate the different perspectives that you had to offer on clerking. Leah, it is especially poignant for me to see your success as you were one of my former research assistants!

I would also like to thank Dean Marc L. Miller at the University of Arizona James E. Rogers College of Law for his continued support for my scholarly endeavors, including the summer research grant to finish this project. And thank you to 2Ls Alexander Brookes and Roberta Lam for your research assistance. You are my target audience, so your thoughts were incredibly valuable! A big thanks also to the UArizona Law Library staff, especially Shaun Esposito and Cynthia Condit who helped me with research questions.

Special thanks are also due to Megan Putler at West Academic. This book is our third project together, and I am constantly impressed with the work of you and your team.

Finally, a huge thanks to my family for their support this summer. In addition to reading every word of this book and catching a few typos, my husband Andrew cooked his fair share of dinners and kept the kids occupied when I needed just another hour to work. And to James and Vera, I know the fact that Mommy writes books isn't very cool right now, especially since there aren't any pictures in them, but I appreciate that you always have hugs and kisses for me when I need a break.

Soli Deo Gloria

Table of Contents

A Short & Happy Guide to Judicial Clerkships

Why Short & Happy

I went to law school on a dare. I had never thought about law school. Didn't know a lawyer. Didn't know a judge. Of course, I knew about Perry Mason because we watched him every weekend. He won every case, and I knew about Thurgood Marshall and the Civil Rights movement because my parents were very active . . . . [A] friend of mine from high school . . . came by my house one day when I was getting my master's and said, "You know, what are you going to do next year?" I said, "Oh, I don't know." He said, "Well, I'm going to law school." We were kind of competitive, so I said, "So am I."

~Judge Ann Claire Williams[1]

The Secret Menu

Sometimes law school seems like the secret menu at a restaurant. If someone lets you in on the secret, a whole panoply of

1   *Judgment Calls with Hon. David F. Levi*, Bolch Judicial Institute Duke Law (Jan. 19, 2021), https://judicialstudies.duke.edu/2021/01/judge-ann-claire-williams-part-1/. Judge Williams was the first Black woman to sit on the United States Court of Appeals for the Seventh Circuit.

meal choices become available. You learn the secret language of the secret menu, which you use when ordering your meal or talking to your other friends in the know. But if no one explains the secret menu to you, you appear woefully uninformed and are stuck with a plain old burger and fries.

Many aspects of the law school experience are similarly mysterious to outsiders. As a first-generation law student from a rural community, I certainly felt that way as a 1L. Growing up, I could count on one hand, using one finger, the number of attorneys that I knew. In many ways, attending an Ivy League law school was more foreign to me than my year living in Eastern Europe right before law school. For example, prior to law school no one explained the importance of signing up for a bar review course or that a law firm party with a "casual attire" dress code did not mean that I could wear jean shorts and a tank top. I think that I avoided committing a serious faux pas, but even twenty years later I look back with chagrin over a few things that I did.

Post-graduation judicial clerkships are part of the secret menu of law school. I am not even sure I knew that clerkships existed before I matriculated, and I clerked after law school because, in part, that is what my 2L and 3L mentors told me to do. The model path for a Harvard Law student was to graduate, clerk for a federal appellate judge, and then go and work for a big law firm. Looking back on my career, I am glad that I followed the advice to clerk, since my clerkship year was fun, rewarding, and highly educational. Incidentally, I am also glad that I did not follow the advice to work for a big law firm and went to work instead for the federal government after my clerkship was over. But that is a story for another book.

Since becoming a law professor a decade ago, I have been on a mission to raise student awareness about post-graduation clerkships and why they are a valuable job experience for students.

But, as I explain in Chapter 1, my knowledge about clerkships was skewed by my experiences. Over the past decade I have learned much about clerkships from talking to judges and hearing what they say about the process. Clerkships aren't just for Ivy League students, and they certainly aren't limited to federal appellate courts. In fact, I think that there is a clerkship out there for nearly every law student—even students who didn't attend an Ivy League law school, didn't graduate at the top of their class, don't want to work in Biglaw, or might want a non-traditional legal career.

This book is designed to be a short, easy to read, and hopefully humorous guide to obtaining a post-graduation clerkship. It is for the students who, like me, were mystified by the law school secret menu. I hope this book unlocks the secret menu of clerkships, demystifies the clerkship process, and opens your eyes to an exciting and rewarding way to start your legal career.

Introduction

I don't have many regrets about my career . . . [b]ut I did one thing really wrong—I didn't clerk after I left law school. . . . [H]aving become a judge, I recognized the mistake I had made. In a year of clerking, you see more about the practice of law than you'll see in 10 years of practice.

~Justice Sonia Sotomayor[1]

Unlocking the Secret Menu

To unlock the secret menu of judicial clerkships you need to ask the right questions. Unfortunately, figuring out the right questions is part of what makes the clerkship process so mysterious. As it turns out, the basis for the right questions comes not from law school but from elementary school.

At some point in elementary school, probably when you were making a poster board report on ants, caterpillars, or your home state, you learned about the 5 W's—the who, what, when, where,

---

[1] Frank Sullivan Jr., *The ABA Judicial Clerkship Program Celebrates Its 10th Anniversary*, 48 JUDGES J. 14, 14 (2009).

and why. Your teacher might have thrown in a lone H—how. Your teacher instructed you to use these questions in connection with writing and information gathering.[2]

As I started thinking about judicial clerkships and the information that I frequently share with students, I realized that I was answering the who, what, when, where, why, and how of judicial clerkships and the application process. So, I decided to organize this book around these questions.

The first question this book will answer is "who?"—who should clerk and who will benefit from the advice in this book? And while I could have made the chapter a single word—"everybody"—I resisted that urge. Instead, in this chapter I explain how potential law students, current law students, recent graduates, law professors, and career service professionals can use the information in this book to understand judicial clerkships and the application process.

"What?" is the next question—what is a judicial clerkship and what types of judicial clerkships are available to law school graduates? Most law students associate the term "judicial clerkship" with federal appellate opportunities. In reality, there are many kinds of judicial clerkships, including federal, state, Tribal, administrative, and international. These clerkships can range from work at a trial court or administrative agency to work at the highest court in a jurisdiction. In short, clerkship opportunities are diverse and wide-ranging.

Next, I will answer the question of "why" a law school graduate should clerk. Although the questions of "when" and "where" usually come next in information gathering, the "why" of clerking can inform the choice of where to clerk. This chapter will explore many of the benefits of clerking and how these benefits are realized at

---

[2]   Summer Steward, *What are the 5 Ws in Writing?—Uses & Examples*, STUDY.COM (Jan. 12, 2022), https://study.com/academy/lesson/what-are-the-5-ws-in-writing-uses-examples.html.

the different types of clerkships. And, because lawyers always want to recognize and address the weaknesses in their own arguments, I will discuss and refute the primary arguments against post-graduation clerkships.

The fourth question is "where?"—where should students clerk? As I mentioned, sometimes this question is answered by looking at "why" a student wants to clerk. If your "why" for clerking is maximum prestige at a national level, then your "where" is rather straightforward—the United States Supreme Court. Beyond the "why," other factors may influence the decision of where to clerk, including a student's academic achievement, geographical limitations, and connections with particular judges. Before you say, "I'm not connected to any judges," I will explain how you can find "connections" in unique places. You might be surprised to learn how playing collegiate water polo, being an Eagle Scout, or being born in a foreign country can connect you to a judge. In the "where" and "how" chapters I will discuss some of these possible connections, how to research judges to draw connections, and how to leverage them in networking and applying to judges.

Finally comes the "how" to apply question. I will discuss the materials you will need for most judicial clerkship applications, including the letters of recommendation, cover letter, and writing sample. This section of the book will be especially helpful to career services offices and law professors writing letters of recommendation because I will share what information judges are looking for in applications and what they find most helpful in letters of recommendation.

If you have been reading carefully up to this point you will notice that I have skipped the question of "when?"—when should you apply? That is, in part, because the "when" varies based on the type and location of the clerkship. For example, different states, and different levels of courts within a state, may have different hiring timelines. You even see judges on the same court having different hiring timelines. Further, even if I went into detail on the timelines for applying, those timelines would probably change, possibly even before the publication of this book!

Take, for example, the federal clerkship hiring process. There have been efforts to regulate the federal clerkship hiring timeline going back to the 1970s.[3] The federal hiring plan that was in place when I graduated from law school was instituted in 2003 and lasted until 2013.[4] At the time of the writing of this book, the current hiring plan been in place since 2018.[5] That plan was extended for two years in 2020.[6] I can't find a formal announcement extending the program a second time, but there is information on the OSCAR[7] website setting applications deadlines through 2024.[8]

To make matters even more complicated, federal judges do not have to follow the federal hiring plan timeline, and many don't. And, that timeline does not apply to recent graduates applying to federal clerkships—they can access OSCAR at anytime.[9]

Before you get too discouraged about timelines, rest assured that I will, to the best of my ability, address timelines in this book. And, because my goal is demystifying the clerkship process, I will

---

[3]   Aaron L. Nielson, *The Future of Federal Law Clerk Hiring*, 98 MARQ. L. REV. 181, 195 (2014).

[4]   *Id.* at 195-202.

[5]   David Lat, *Order In The Court, Order In The Court: The Law Clerk Hiring Plan Returns!*, ABOVE THE LAW (Mar. 1, 2018, 7:43 PM), https://abovethelaw.com/2018/03/order-in-the-court-the-law-clerk-hiring-plan-returns/.

[6]   David Barron et al., *Ad Hoc Committee on Law Clerk Hiring*, ONLINE SYSTEM FOR CLERKSHIP APPLICATIONS AND REVIEW (Oct. 2, 2020), https://oscar.uscourts.gov/assets/Federal_Law_Clerk_Hiring_Plan_Two-Year_Extension.pdf.

[7]   OSCAR stands for the "Online Systems for Clerkship Applications and Review." It is managed by the Administrative Office of the United States Courts and is used for federal clerkship applications at both the trial and appellate levels. *About OSCAR*, ONLINE SYSTEM FOR CLERKSHIP APPLICATION AND REVIEW, https://oscar.uscourts.gov/about (last visited Jun. 20, 2022).

[8]   *Federal Law Clerk Hiring Plan*, ONLINE SYSTEM FOR CLERKSHIP APPLICATION AND REVIEW (Apr. 19, 2022), https://oscar.uscourts.gov/federal_law_clerk_hiring_pilot.

[9]   *Id.*

empower you with tools to find answers to the "when" question so your clerkship applications are timely.

The final chapter of this book explores how to make the most of your clerkship year, including giving back to your law school community, networking with co-clerks and your judge, and understanding your ethical responsibilities as a clerk. I will also discuss "stacking" clerkships for graduates who want multiple clerkship experiences.

I hope you find this guide helpful as you start your journey toward finding a judicial clerkship. Let's get started.

CHAPTER 1

WHO Should Clerk?

My clerkship with Judge Diana Murphy influenced greatly the way that I approach my role as a judge and how I work with my clerks. I had the chance to experience close-up how a superb judge runs a courtroom, writes a well-reasoned opinion, and deals respectfully with counsel, litigants, and court personnel.

~Justice Margaret Chutich[1]

There is an easy answer to the question "Who should clerk?"—"Everyone," or at least all law school graduates.

I believe there is a judicial clerkship for every law school graduate and every graduate can benefit from clerking.

While not every student is suited for every type of clerkship, and not every type of clerkship is suited for every student, if we look broadly at the types of clerkships available and the benefits of clerking, we can match graduates with a personally and professionally rewarding clerkship experience.

---

[1] Jon Schmidt, *An Interview with Justice Margaret Chutich of the Minnesota Supreme Court*, 73 BENCH & B. MINN. 32 (2016).

This perspective challenges the status quo that most law professors experienced when they were students. Let me explain.

Nearly 95% of law professors at top-ten law schools, and well over 50% of law professors at lower-ranked schools, attended top-ten schools.[2] A staggering "11% of all law professors at American law schools are [Harvard Law School] graduates."[3]

Where do students from top-ten schools clerk? Typically, at the federal level, including the United States Supreme Court, federal circuit courts of appeal, and federal district courts. Between 2016 and 2020, Harvard Law School sent, on average, 109 students each year to clerk at federal appellate courts.[4] This amounts to nearly one-fifth of its graduating class.[5] In contrast, only about 23 Harvard Law graduates each year clerked for state supreme courts, and only about four graduates clerked for other state courts.[6] During the same time period, the University of Chicago Law School sent, on average, 48 graduates—or one-fourth of its graduating class—to federal appellate courts and only about seven graduates to state appellate courts.[7]

Why are these statistics important? Well, the statistics are important because your law professors probably have a top-ten law school view of clerkships—a view primarily focused on federal

---

[2]   Eric J. Segall & Adam Feldman, *The Elite Teaching the Elite: Who Gets Hired by the Top Law Schools?*, 68 J. LEGAL EDUC. 614, 616 (2019).

[3]   *Law Teaching*, HARVARD LAW SCH., https://hls.harvard.edu/dept/oaa/law-teaching/ (last visited Jun. 20, 2022).

[4]   *Judicial Clerkships from HLS*, HARVARD LAW SCH., https://hls.harvard.edu/dept/ocs/judicial-clerkships-from-hls/ (last visited Jun. 20, 2022).

[5]   Harvard Law generally admits around 550 to 560 students each year. *See, e.g., HLS Profile and Facts*, HARVARD LAW SCH., https://hls.harvard.edu/dept/jdadmissions/apply-to-harvard-law-school/hls-profile-and-facts/ (last visited Jun. 28, 2022).

[6]   *Id.*

[7]   *Judicial Clerkships*, UNIV. OF CHI. LAW SCH., https://www.law.uchicago.edu/clerkships (last visited Jun. 20, 2022). Chicago Law School admits around 190 students a year. *See, e.g., JD Class Profile*, UNIV. OF CHI. LAW SCH., https://www.law.uchicago.edu/class-profile (last visited Jun. 28, 2022).

appellate clerkships. And while federal appellate clerkships can be a great experience and a prestigious credential, there aren't that many federal appellate clerkship positions available—especially if Harvard is placing over 100 federal appellate clerks each year.

There are only 179 authorized judgeships on the federal appellate bench,[8] with most judges taking three to four clerks each year. That is slightly over 700 positions with active judges. Although this number excludes senior judges, who still take cases and often hire clerks, you get the point—there are not that many federal appellate clerkship spots available. If you include lower federal courts, there are approximately 1,700 judges in the federal system.[9] Assuming that each of these judges hires 2.5 clerks (likely an overestimate) that means that there is a *total* of 4,250 federal clerk positions each year.[10] In 2021, however, 35,287 students graduated from American law schools.[11]

But, before you get too discouraged, remember what I wrote at the beginning of this chapter—"I believe there is a judicial clerkship for every law school graduate." That means you (if you are a law student). These clerkships can be found on other courts, like the state courts. There are approximately 30,000 state court judges.[12] Assuming each of these judges takes one clerk a year

---

[8]   *U.S. Courts of Appeals Additional Authorized Judgeships*, ADMIN. OFFICE OF THE UNITED STATES COURTS, https://www.uscourts.gov/sites/default/files/appealsauth.pdf (last visited Jun. 20, 2022).

[9]   *FAQs: Judges in the United States*, UNIV. OF DENVER: INST. FOR THE ADVANCEMENT OF THE AM. LEGAL SYS. 3 (June 12, 2014), https://iaals.du.edu/sites/default/files/documents/publications/judge_faq.pdf.

[10]   This is almost certainly an overestimate. Most district court judges take only two clerks, and some of these judges only hire clerks every other year. Federal magistrate judges generally hire anywhere between zero and two clerks.

[11]   Statista Research Department, *Number of law graduates in the United States from 2013 to 2021*, STATISTA (Apr. 29, 2022), https://www.statista.com/statistics/428985/number-of-law-graduates-us/#:~:text=Numberöf%20law%20graduatesïn%20theÜ.S.%202013"2021&text=Asöf%202021'%2035'287%20students,schoolïn%20the Ünited%20States.

[12]   *FAQs: Judges in the United States*, UNIV. OF DENVER: INST. FOR THE ADVANCEMENT OF THE AM. LEGAL SYS. 3 (June 12, 2014), https://iaals.du.edu/sites/default/files/documents/publications/judge_faq.pdf.

(maybe an overestimate), that means 30,000 clerk positions.[13] Add in administrative clerkships, international opportunities, and Tribal clerkships, and you have lots of opportunities, enough for each law school graduate.

We will discuss the different types of clerkships available and how to select the right one in the next few chapters.

Getting Started

Some law students start thinking about clerkships before they even apply to law school. And while that is great, especially if you want to secure an ultra-competitive clerkship, my experience has been that those students are few and far between (and rarely the ones who end up in my office asking for help). Students farther along in their law school education, however, can still secure a clerkship. In short, it isn't too late for even the 3Ls or recent graduates to start applying to clerkships!

Let's look at what you should be doing at each stage of your law school career to position yourself for a clerkship.

Prospective Law Students

It was in the summer of my thirteenth year that my career goals were unalterably fixed. I knew I wanted to be a judge. . . . Almost every day that summer, I would take a bus to Calvert and Fayette Streets in downtown Baltimore and spend the day listening to cases presented

---

[13] This is probably an overestimate, since some state judges might not have clerks, or they might share clerks. In Arizona, some of our trial judges have a single clerk, others don't. In Virginia, five or six trial judges share a single clerk.

> *to the judges of the Supreme Bench of Baltimore, now*
> *the Circuit Court of Baltimore City.*

~Judge Dana M. Levitz[14]

So you want to go to law school? Great! You will learn a lot and meet some amazing people. You also want to clerk for the United States Supreme Court? Ok, that is a pretty tough gig to get.

Because so many aspects of judicial clerkships are part of the secret law school menu, as a prospective law student, you might not understand how things like law school rank, student activities, and GPA can impact your chances of securing certain clerkships—especially very competitive clerkships. You also might not fully understand the types of clerkships that are available and the benefits these different clerkships offer. While clerking at the United States Supreme Court definitely seems cool, if you want to be a trial attorney, you will benefit from a federal district court clerkship, which is far more attainable.

This book will help you understand the array of judicial clerkship options, the benefits of the different types of judicial clerkships, the credentials generally required for those different types of clerkships, and ways to bolster your clerkship applications. This information can help you make informed decisions about where to go to law school, what courses to take while in law school, and what activities to do while in law school.

1Ls

> *I knew I wanted to be a judge even before I became a*
> *lawyer. After my first year of law school, I interned for*
> *Judge Henry Werker in the Southern District of New York.*
> *I loved the experience—I saw some trials, including a bank*

---

[14] Dana M. Levitz, *So, You Think You Want to Be a Judge*, 38 U. BALTIMORE L. REV. 57, 58 (2008).

robbery trial; I drafted some opinions for the judge; and I saw justice in action. I decided that someday I would come back and be a judge myself.

~Judge Denny Chin[15]

Welcome to law school! As a first-year student you have a lot of things to figure out, like who should be in your study group, how and when to brief cases for class, and what student groups to join. Amid all these decisions will be a question that you will hear often: What do you want to do when you graduate? As you know by now, I want your answer to be: to clerk.

The 1L year is an ideal time to start thinking about clerkships. Like the prospective students, you should take time to learn about the different types of clerkships. You should carefully consider why you want to clerk and the benefits the different clerkships offer. In addition to reading this book, you can help yourself answer these questions by talking to upper-class mentors, alumni, professors, and career services professionals. Talking to professors also alerts them to your interest in a clerkship position, which can help you make connections to judges and receive strong letters of recommendation.

If you want a more competitive clerkship, like a federal clerkship or state supreme court clerkship, you should focus on getting good grades, taking the right classes, and writing on to law review or another journal. Another great clerkship credential is working as a research assistant for a professor. You can fine-tune your writing and secure a great letter of recommendation in the process! While this might all seem a bit overwhelming and a lot of work, starting now will make it easier when you apply!

---

[15]   Rachel Pereira, *Four Federal Judges Talk about Their Journey to the Bench*, AMERICAN BAR ASSOCIATION (Feb. 12, 2019), https://www.americanbar.org/groups/litigation/committees/diversity-inclusion/articles/2019/winter2019-four-federal-judges-talk-about-their-journey-to-the-bench/.

2Ls

> *[A] successful candidate will have demonstrated sound, professional writing skills. Beyond that and the other important information (like academic background, law-related work experience, etc.) to stand out from the crowd as a unique individual, applicants should emphasize the breadth of their interests, and include something that will become thematic . . . such as any language proficiencies (i.e., fluent in French), interesting hobbies (i.e., parasailing), work-ethic indicators (i.e., worked self through college and law school at Applebees), charitable passions (i.e., helped build a Habitat for Humanity house), talents (i.e., writes poetry), etc.*

~Judge Annette J. Scieszinski[16]

If your first year in law school teaches you how to be a law student, second year teaches you how to be a lawyer. Life as a 2L can be extra challenging for students—not only do you have a more sporadic, less structured class schedule, but you are now taking on leadership roles in student organizations and working on academic journals. You might even be juggling a job or internship.

The 2L year is an important one for judicial clerkships. Under the current federal hiring plan, students apply for most federal clerkships at the end of their 2L year. Many state courts follow a similar timeline, with deadlines in the spring and summer of the 2L year. Federal judges who don't follow the federal hiring plan might look at applications as soon as the start of your 2L year. This means that if you want to clerk for one of these judges, you will need to

---

[16]   Darhiana Mateo Tellez, *Clerkship Confidential*, 43 Student Law. 28, 32 (2015).

contact their chambers over the summer between your 1L and 2L years to learn their application deadlines.

Clerkship application deadlines that don't fall during the 2L year, often fall at the very start of the 3L year. For example, if you want to apply for an administrative court clerkship through the Department of Justice Honors Program (DOJ Honors), that deadline is currently at the end of the 2L summer.

Because most clerkship applications are due during or at the end of the 2L year, the 2L year is also your prime opportunity to take those challenging classes that judges like to see on your resume, develop a writing sample, participate in student organizations, and network. I will discuss this all in greater detail in Chapter 6.

Because, the 2L year is pivotal for clerkship applications, if you haven't tackled the questions of why and where you want to clerk, you should start that process now. This includes researching judges and ascertaining timelines and application requirements. It also means you must build your application package, which typically consists of letters of recommendation, a cover letter, your resume, a law school transcript, and a writing sample. I will discuss application materials in more detail in Chapter 5.

3Ls

> *[S]tudents should include things in the cover letter or resume that show they are smart, e.g., outstanding performances in particular classes, success in activities like moot court, strong undergraduate academic record, etc.*
>
> ~Judge Frank Sullivan, Jr.[17]

---

[17]   *Id.*

Hey 3Ls, it isn't too late to think about clerkships. In fact, I once had a student reach out to me for the first time about clerking at the end of his 3L year. That same day, a former student who was leaving a state intermediate appellate clerkship emailed me to tell me that his judge had an open position. I was able to connect the recent graduate with that open position in about a week, and he was offered the job. Now, like the stories told in diet plan commercials, that type of result is not typical. But, that type of result is possible, if you do the work.

If you haven't thought about clerkships before your 3L year, you will spend much of this year playing catch-up. You will need to research judges, courts, and application deadlines. You will also need to gather your application materials, including reaching out to professors and employers for letters of recommendation.

What types of clerkship opportunities will be available for you? Some state intermediate appellate and trial courts have application deadlines during the 3L year. In addition to the standard clerkship timelines for 3Ls, other clerkship opportunities may arise. New judges are appointed, confirmed, or elected to courts, and sometimes clerks leave positions unexpectedly, like in my example above. Thus, you will need to keep an eye out for new judges or positions that open up outside of the normal timelines. If you aren't able to secure a clerkship, please read on. There are excellent clerkship opportunities available to recent graduates too.

Recent(ish) Graduates

> *Most of my hires are people that have prior experience between law school and my clerkship, be that a district clerkship, a year of practice, or something of the like.*

~Judge Catharina Haynes[18]

Maybe you didn't want to clerk when you graduated from law school or felt like your application wasn't strong enough for the more competitive clerkships. Maybe you clerked at the trial level and now you want an appellate clerkship, or maybe you clerked at the state level and now, after a few years of practice, you want to do a federal clerkship. Maybe you are working at a firm in California, but you really want to live in Florida. Clerkships are a great way to make a career transition! One example of this—you generally do not have to pass the bar exam before clerking. This means that you could obtain a clerkship in Florida, move there, and study for the bar while clerking.

I have seen recent(ish) graduates use clerkships for career transitions, including geographic transitions or transitions into a different type of practice area. I have also seen students work for a few years to bolster their credentials and make themselves stronger applicants for more competitive clerkships.

There are lots of benefits to clerking after a few years in practice. For example, you bring a stronger skill set than a fresh graduate. As the quote above shows, some judges prefer to hire clerks with prior legal work experience, such as a prior clerkship or a few years of practice. Recent graduates applying for clerkships also aren't subject to the federal hiring plan, even for judges who follow the plan. Thus, they can apply at any time, making them a

---

[18] JUDICIAL CLERKSHIP FORUM: A CONVERSATION WITH 12 JUDGES, AMERICAN BAR ASSOCIATION JUDICIAL DIVISION LAWYERS CONFERENCE 16 (2015).

better fit for new judges who are confirmed, appointed, or elected to the bench off the regular clerkship cycle.

Professors

> *I had professors who thought I did well enough in their classes and were looking out for me . . . .*

~Justice Maria Araujo Kahn[19]

A funny thing started happening to me a few years ago, when I was about fifteen years out of law school, and it continues today. My law school classmates started becoming judges. They are federal judges and state judges, trial judges and appellate judges.

Now, if I were a glass-half-empty person, I might feel like a big underachiever. But I view it as a glass half full—look at all the potential clerkship opportunities for my students! And, as both my students and my judge friends will tell you, I am not afraid to call, text, email, and message my judge friends about potential clerks.

I look to not only former classmates and colleagues who are now on the bench for potential student clerkship placements, I also look at the judges that I regularly interface with in my academic position or other organizations. Many of these judges have become friends. They reach out to me when they have a clerkship opening, and I reach out to them if my students are applying for clerkships. I am honest with the judges about my students' abilities—which helps build trust with the judges and ensures that my students find positions that match their skills and interests.

The point of this isn't to show what cool friends I have; the point is to show why professors should read this book. We can

---

[19] Justice Kahn, who serves on the Connecticut Supreme Court, was discussing two professors who encouraged her to apply for a clerkship. Erin Degregorio, *Judicial Center Initiative Welcomes First Generation Judges to Share Insights*, FORDHAM LAW NEWS (Feb. 25, 2020), https://news.law.fordham.edu/blog/2020/02/25/judicial-center-initiative-welcomes-first-generation-judges-to-share-insights/.

leverage our connections to help our students get clerkships. But, to do that effectively, we need to know what types of clerkships exist (meaning not just federal appellate clerkships), the benefits of clerkships for our students, and how to help our students research and apply for the right clerkships.

Career Services Professionals

Working in a law school career services office is hard. Your offices are often understaffed, but your results are highly scrutinized. You must be experts in all sorts of possible employment opportunities—including employment opportunities that you haven't experienced firsthand.

I hope that this book will be a great resource to you, especially if you haven't clerked. As career services professionals, you can help your students find clerkships by building connections with students who are clerking, with alumni who are judges, and with local judges who might want to hire your graduates. You can also identify helpful members of the faculty who will advocate for students and build deeper connections in the judiciary. Hopefully, this book will give you some ideas on building a clerkship culture at your institution, which will raise your students' profile and the profile of your school for years to come.

Short & Happy!

- There is a clerkship for every student!
- Know that your law professors might have a federally-skewed view of clerkships.
- The sooner you start thinking about clerkships the better, but even 3Ls and recent graduates can find clerkship opportunities.
- Law professors can play an important role in encouraging students to clerk.

CHAPTER 2

WHAT Is a Judicial Clerkship?

Every chambers, and every judge, will use clerks in a different way. The way that I use law clerks is generally as really colleagues. Really try to work as a team. They will do research; I will do research. They will write; I will write. They edit my work; I edit their work. . . . We all basically do the same thing.

~Judge Robert Bacharach[1]

What Is a Judicial Clerkship?

If you are already in law school, you know that the words "law clerk" get bandied about a lot. The words may describe summer positions at law firms, non-profit organizations, and government offices. They may also be used to describe internships or externships with a judge during law school. Although these experiences are valuable, they are not the focus of this book and not how I use "law clerk" in the context of a "judicial clerkship."

---

[1] Life at Harvard Law, *Judge Gives Clerkship Advice*, YOUTUBE, 0:20-0:45 (Nov. 28, 2021), https://www.youtube.com/watch?v=_1NPEFRk_4w.

This book is focused on post-graduation, term judicial clerkships. Let me unpack that definition. First, these are positions for law students who have graduated with a J.D. from an ABA accredited law school or will have graduated when the clerkship begins, but that isn't a hard and fast rule. For example, under the current federal hiring plan it appears that someone who is a "law school graduate" and also holds an LLM degree from an ABA accredited school meets the "minimum qualifications for law clerks," as does someone who, "in the opinion of the judge," has "[d]emonstrated proficiency in legal studies" equivalent to the other minimum qualifications listed.[2] I assume this means that someone who "reads the law"—like Kim Kardashian—would qualify.[3] State courts have their own requirements, although if you have graduated from an ABA accredited law school you likely meet those qualifications.

Judges often hire law school graduates regardless of bar passage. Most often, law clerks take the bar before they start a clerkship and are waiting for bar results when they begin their term clerkships. But, for many judges, you might not even be required to take the bar exam to be employed as a law clerk.

Second, this book is focused on term judicial clerkships. Generally, term judicial clerkships last for one or two years. This is true at both the state and federal level. Some judges have a career (permanent) law clerk in addition to term clerks. And some judges have only career clerks. While career clerks and term clerks generally do the same work, career clerks stay in their positions for longer than one or two years and often help the judge manage and

---

[2]   *Qualifications, Salary, and Benefits*, ONLINE SYS. FOR CLERKSHIP APPLICATION AND REV., https://oscar.uscourts.gov/qualifications_salary_benefits#qualifications (last visited July 20, 2022).

[3]   Debra Cassens Weiss, *Students try to avoid law school costs with 'reading law' path to law license*, ABAJOURNAL (Jul. 30, 2014, 5:53 PM), https://www.abajournal.com/news/article/want_to_avoid_the_costs_of_law_school_these_students_try_reading_law_path_t.

review the work of the term clerks. Career clerks can also play an important role in the hiring of term clerks. Additionally, career clerks may take the lead on complex cases that come before the court, help the judge with "extracurricular" activities like speeches or law review articles, and may assist more with administrative tasks.

Before I discuss the work that clerks do, it is worth mentioning one other type of attorney that works at many courthouses—staff attorneys. Unlike term clerks and career clerks who work for a specific judge, staff attorneys usually work for the clerk of the court's office or a specific staff attorney office. Staff attorneys perform similar tasks to law clerks—they research and review cases and draft legal opinions. In some courts they may handle specific types of cases—such as cases not set for oral argument, habeas cases, immigration cases, or child protective services cases. Staff attorney positions, like career clerk positions, are often long-term career positions, although some states or federal jurisdictions may offer a term staff attorney position.[4] Term law clerks may transition into a career law clerk or staff attorney position when the term clerk position with a particular judge ends.

Now that we have covered what judicial law clerks aren't, let's talk about what they are—or rather what they do. The specifics vary by court and even by judge, but I can provide a general overview.

---

[4] *See, e.g., Office of Staff Counsel,* United States Court of Appeals for the Fourth Circuit, https://www.ca4.uscourts.gov/docs/pdfs/staffattorneyvacancy announcement2020.pdf?sfvrsn=c163b809_2#:~:text=POSITION%20SUMMARY%3A&text= Staffättorneys%20will%20beäppointed%20toöne"year%20term%20positions (last visited Aug. 3, 2022).

Appellate Clerkships

The relationship between judges and clerks is both close and critical.

~Senior Judge Michael Daly Hawkins[5]

At the appellate level, state and federal law clerks perform the same general type of work. This work largely consists of reviewing cases before a set of judges. Judges typically divide cases up among their law clerks. For each case, a law clerk will review the record and the briefs, research the law in the area, and write a bench memorandum. In general, the bench memorandum sets out the issues on appeal in the case, the arguments of the parties, an analysis of those arguments based on independent research, a recommendation for the judge on how to decide the case, and possible questions for oral argument.[6]

Usually, the judge and law clerk then discuss the case—a lot! For some chambers this might resemble an oral argument, with the judge asking the law clerk and the other clerks questions about the case, especially in the days leading up to oral argument. Clerks usually attend the oral arguments, which may require travel from the judge's duty station to a central courthouse. After oral argument, clerks help judges draft opinions, concurrences, or dissents from the cases decided at oral argument. In the federal system, this cycle repeats about every four to six weeks, perhaps with a longer break over the summer.

This description, of course, varies by judge and court. Some judges don't have clerks write bench memoranda. Other judges

---

[5]   Michael Daly Hawkins, *Clerks in the Time of Coronavirus (with Apologies to Gabriel García Márquez)*, 21 J. App. Prac. & Process 225, 225 (2021).

[6]   Jessica Klarfeld, *The Bench Memorandum*, The Writing Ctr., Georgetown Univ. Law Ctr. (2011). https://www.law.georgetown.edu/wp-content/uploads/2018/07/The-Bench-Memorandum-Jessica-Klarfeld-2011.pdf.

prefer to prepare their own opinions, or at least the first drafts. Some appellate courts rarely hold oral argument.

The life and work of an appellate judge is often isolated. They work individually in chambers, sometimes a great distance from the main court building where oral argument is held, and even from other judges. This dynamic often results in a close working relationship between judges and law clerks. Law clerks serve as their judges' confidants and sounding boards. This is especially true at courts where the judges don't discuss cases with other judges before oral argument. In many instances, a judge's law clerks become like a second family. For example, when I clerked for a federal appellate judge, our chambers frequently went out to lunch together and we chatted about everything from our cases to sports. I also have friends who attend regular law clerk reunions with their judge and all the judge's former clerks. As I will discuss in Chapter 3, this close mentoring relationship and broader clerkship family is one reason to clerk.

District (Trial) Court Clerkships

Indeed, having served in recent years as both a trial and appellate judge, I always tell students what is now a statement against interest: working for a trial court will teach them more things they did not learn in law school.

~Judge Gregg Costa[7]

Like appellate law clerks, federal district court law clerks spend significant time researching cases and drafting orders and opinions. But unlike their appellate counterparts, they also spend significant time in court. Where federal appellate judges might travel for oral argument every four to six weeks, federal district

---

[7]   Greg Costa, *Clerking to Excess? The Case Against Second (and Third and Fourth) Clerkships*, 102 JUDICATURE 24 (2018).

court judges can preside over multiple criminal and civil hearings a day and multi-week trials. This difference means that federal district court clerks take a more active role in actual court proceedings. This also means that some of their research must be completed under tight deadlines, especially if it relates to issues that may arise in an ongoing trial, like questions related to objections, evidentiary issues, or jury charges. In sum, federal district court clerkships are faster-paced than appellate clerkships.

State trial court clerkships are even more fast-paced than federal district court clerkships. Although it certainly varies by state and even by type of court, state trial court clerks do less research and writing and much more trial management. Some state court trial judges, like judges on a family, juvenile, or criminal court, spend most of their time in court, and their clerks will do the same—assisting with the docket or researching issues that arise. Not all state court trial judges have clerks, and in some courts multiple judges share a single clerk.

What Types of Clerkships Are out There?

I think clerking is priceless and invaluable. With very few exceptions, any law student should seriously pursue opportunities to serve as a clerk for one or two years.

~Judge Andre Davis[8]

Now that we have looked generally at what judicial clerks do, let's look in more detail at different kinds of judicial clerkships.

But first, it is important to generally understand the main court systems in the United States. The court structure in the federal system and in most state systems is triparted, consisting of a trial

---

[8]   JUDICIAL CLERKSHIP FORUM: A CONVERSATION WITH 12 JUDGES, AMERICAN BAR ASSOCIATION JUDICIAL DIVISION LAWYERS CONFERENCE 7 (2015).

court, an intermediate appellate court, and a supreme court.[9] Generally, parties have an appeal of right from the trial court to the intermediate appellate court, which means that the intermediate appellate court must hear their case. Parties then have a discretionary appeal from the intermediate appellate court to the highest court in a jurisdiction, which means that the highest court doesn't have to hear the appeal.

In the federal court system, there is no further appeal after the United States Supreme Court. In the state court system, cases involving federal law and the Constitution, including cases about whether a state law or constitution might violate the United States Constitution, can be appealed to the United States Supreme Court.[10] The two court systems operate independently, although some cases that originate in state court can ultimately end up in the federal court system if the cases raise federal issues, and vice versa if a federal case is really based on state law.

I have illustrated this in the graphics below.

Federal Court System

---

[9]   Currently, forty-one states have state intermediate appellate courts. *See generally The Role of State Intermediate Appellate Courts*, NAT'L CTR. FOR STATE CTS. (Nov.   2012),   https://www.sji.gov/wp/wp-content/uploads/Report_5_CCJSCA_ Report.pdf; *List of State Intermediate Appellate Courts*, WIKIPEDIA, https://en. wikipedia.org/wiki/List_of_state_intermediate_appellate_courts (last visited July 20, 2022).

[10]   28 U.S.C. § 1257.

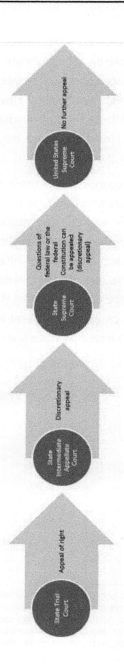

State Court System

State Trial Court — Appeal of right — State Intermediate Appellate Court — Discretionary appeal — State Supreme Court — Questions of federal law or the federal Constitution can be appealed (discretionary appeal) — United States Supreme Court — No further appeal

These graphics of the federal and state court systems, however, only tell part of the story. In addition to these court systems, there are Tribal courts, military courts, specialty courts, intergovernmental courts, and federal or state administrative courts that adjudicate cases. All of these types of court potentially offer clerkships.

Now let's look specifically at the types of clerkships available. Warning, the rest of this chapter gets pretty technical. I encourage you to press on so that you can see the breadth of clerkship opportunities available.

United States Supreme Court[11]

I debated whether I should include a section on United States Supreme Court (SCOTUS) clerkships given how rare and difficult these clerkships are to secure. In fact, only thirty-six law school graduates clerk for SCOTUS each year. But, since my goal is to demystify the process, I thought it only right to discuss this holy grail of judicial clerkships.

Successful SCOTUS clerkship applicants are generally top graduates from top law schools. If you look at lists of past, current, and future clerks, you will see that most of them graduated from just a handful of law schools—Harvard, Yale, Chicago, and Stanford.[12] Similarly, most of the successful applicants completed one or two previous clerkships, usually federal clerkships, for what are called "feeder judges"—judges who frequently send former

---

[11] For an older, but still relevant, look at the Supreme Court clerkship process, there is an ABA Journal Podcast episode that looks in detail at the process. ABA Journal Podcast, *Lucky 36: What It Takes to Land a Supreme Court Clerkship*, ABA JOURNAL (Oct. 1. 2012), https://www.abajournal.com/news/article/podcast_monthly_episode _31.

[12] Wikipedia is a great resource for finding clerk lists. *Lists of Law Clerks of the Supreme Court of the United States*, WIKIPEDIA, https://en.wikipedia.org/wiki/Lists _of_law_clerks_of_the_Supreme_Court_of_the_United_States (last visited July 20, 2022).

clerks to SCOTUS. Thus, to clerk at the Supreme Court level you need to get the "right" lower court clerkships.

There are certainly exceptions. For example, lower-ranked schools like Pepperdine, Florida, Mississippi, and BYU have sent graduates to clerk at the Supreme Court. Also, Professor Tara Helfman, who graduated from Yale Law School in 2006 and did not clerk for any judge after law school, was selected by Justice Neil Gorsuch to clerk for the 2022-2023 term.[13] But, despite these few exceptions, being a top student from a top law school and clerking for a prominent feeder judge is the most likely path to a SCOTUS clerkship.

Another way to improve your chances of clerking at SCOTUS is to befriend or work for a former SCOTUS clerk who can recommend you to their Justice. These former SCOTUS clerks might be your law school professors or partners at law firms where you were a summer associate.

Most SCOTUS clerks have made it a career ambition since before law school to clerk on the Supreme Court. They focus all their energies on this goal and work all of their potential connections to achieve it.

What do SCOTUS clerks do? Much of their work resembles the work of other appellate court clerks—they write bench memoranda on cases set for oral argument and help draft opinions, concurrences, and dissents. Because most of the cases that come before SCOTUS are ones that the Court has discretion to hear, clerks also write recommendation memos to the Justices on whether the Court should take cases in the first place. Some of the Justices participate in the "cert pool," where their chambers share memos on whether to take cases, lessening the burden for those clerks.

---

[13] *Lists of Law Clerks of the Supreme Court of the United States (Seat 9),* WIKIPEDIA, https://en.wikipedia.org/wiki/List_of_law_clerks_of_the_Supreme_Court_of_the_United_States_(Seat_9) (last visited July 20, 2022).

Other Justices don't. Finally, clerks may help field emergency motions or petitions that come before SCOTUS, like a stay of execution in a death penalty case.

SCOTUS clerks, upon completion of their clerkships, are highly sought after in practice. Some law firms offer former clerks signing bonuses of up to $450,000.[14]

Federal Appellate

> *I still remember when I was sworn in [to the Fifth Circuit] . . . almost eleven years ago, the judge who I had clerked for . . . told me, reflecting on his career, that the best part of being a Fifth Circuit judge was working with the law clerks. . . . I agree that working with clerks is the best part of the job, because you're working with young, eager legal minds who have done very well in law school. It is just a joy to work with such people.*

~Judge Leslie H. Southwick[15]

If a SCOTUS clerkship is the holy grail of clerkships, then a federal appellate clerkship is like finding a four-leaf clover. It is possible, but it requires a lot of work. As I discussed in Chapter 1, there are only 179 active federal appellate judgeships in the United States. These judges generally hire three to four clerks each year. Additionally, some senior federal appellate judges hire clerks. But, overall there is a small number of federal appellate clerkships out there, and as I also discussed in Chapter 1, a large number of those clerkships go to students from the top-ten law schools. There are exceptions, of course, and some federal appellate judges are willing

---

[14]   Staci Zaretsky, *Elite Biglaw Firms Likely To Offer $450K In Signing Bonuses To Supreme Court Clerks*, ABOVE THE LAW (July 14, 2021, 10:47 AM), https://abovethe law.com/2021/07/elite-biglaw-firms-likely-to-offer-450k-in-signing-bonuses-to-supreme-court-clerks/.

[15]   Victoria A. Lowery, *Interview with Judge Leslie H. Southwick*, 37 MISS. C. L. REV. 32, 38-39 (2018).

to consider applications from lower-ranked schools. In Chapter 4 I will discuss ways to find those exceptions.

What do federal appellate clerks do? As I discussed above, much of their work involves researching cases set for oral argument and writing bench memoranda on those cases, which set out the facts of the case, the arguments of the parties, the relevant law, and a tentative decision.

Given the heavy emphasis on research and writing, federal appellate clerkships are a great job opportunity for students who either like that type of work or want to have an appellate practice. But—FYI—if you don't like researching and writing, you probably don't want to have an appellate practice.

As an appellate clerk, you typically have sufficient time to dive deeply into each case since each clerk typically handles only a few cases per argument cycle. The frequency of oral argument varies by circuit, and you can generally find the oral argument schedule on each federal appellate court's website.

Like the lifestyle of an appellate judge, the lifestyle of appellate clerks might seem a bit too solitary for some people. Generally, ethical limitations only permit you to discuss cases with your co-clerks and the judge, and, apart from oral argument, you might have little interaction with other judges and clerks. This is especially true if the judge's duty station or home chambers is far from the main courthouse.

When I clerked on the Fourth Circuit, we traveled from my judge's home chambers in South Carolina, to Richmond, Virginia for oral argument. Because the entire Fourth Circuit met the same week in Richmond for oral argument, I did get to meet other judges and clerks during "court week." But, in some federal circuits, like the Ninth Circuit, the oral argument panels are dispersed across the circuit, and it is rare for the full court to assemble in the same location.[16]

The close chambers working environment makes "fit" an important hiring consideration—perhaps even the *most* important hiring consideration—for many judges. Judges want to hire clerks who will fit well into their chambers family. Thus, the interview is critical for federal appellate clerkships. Applicants often interview with the judge and the current clerks, and interface with the judicial assistant. All of this is intentional. If a judge has a career clerk and administrative staff, those people probably have a significant voice in the hiring process.

What qualifications do you need to clerk at the federal appellate level? Like most answers in law school, it depends. Some of the qualifications depend on what the individual judge requires, while others depend on the law school that you graduate from. For example, many judges prefer students who graduate in the top five to ten percent of their graduating class. But, as I noted in Chapter 1, approximately one-fourth of the graduating class at Chicago secures a federal appellate clerkship, which means that the ten percent rule doesn't apply at Chicago, or other top law schools. I think that a good rule of thumb is the higher-ranked your law school, the less your particular class rank matters. If you graduate from a lower ranked or unranked law school, graduating at the very top of your class is critical to be competitive for federal appellate clerkships.

In addition to graduating near the top of your class, most federal appellate judges prefer their applicants to have experience working on a student-edited journal, with some judges preferring work on the primary journal at the law school, such as the law review. Finally, federal appellate judges are increasingly preferring

---

[16] This is especially true since the Ninth Circuit does not hold traditional en banc arguments.

candidates who have completed a prior clerkship, such as a federal district court clerkship or a state appellate clerkship.

In terms of prestige, federal appellate clerkships fall right below SCOTUS clerkships. Federal appellate clerkships are marketable nationwide, with some firms offering signing bonuses of up to $125,000 for associates who have completed a one-year federal clerkship.[17] Most large law firms, however, have bonuses under the $100,000 mark, although incoming associates can negotiate "stacked" bonuses for multiple clerkships.[18]

When should you apply for federal appellate clerkships? Under the current federal clerkship hiring plan, students can access OSCAR near the start of their 2L spring semester. Judges following the federal hiring plan accept applications, conduct interviews, and hire in early June immediately following a student's 2L year. Of course, as I have mentioned before, not all judges follow the federal hiring plan. Anecdotally, I know that some of these judges start reviewing applications in the fall of a student's 2L year.

Federal District (Trial) Court

> *The Herculean task of reading and deciding at the district court is almost impossible without the aid of law clerks. Because the reading and writing of the district court is cabined both by time constraints and the volume of material to be consumed, the law clerk becomes central to this process.*
>
> ~Judge Donald W. Molloy[19]

---

[17] Kathryn Rubino, *Elite Law Firm Will Offer $150,000 in Clerkship Bonuses*, ABOVE THE LAW (April 26, 2022, 12:16 PM), https://abovethelaw.com/2022/04/elite-law-firm-will-offer-150000-in-clerkship-bonuses/.

[18] *Id.*

[19] Donald W. Molloy, *Designated Hitters, Pinch Hitters, and Bat Boys: Judges Dealing with Judgment and Inexperience, Career Clerks Or Term Clerks*, 82 LAW & CONTEMP. PROBS. 133, 135 (2019).

It is hard to compare federal appellate and federal district court clerkships. Fundamentally, the two experiences are quite different, and this is because clerks see cases at different stages in the litigation process. Federal district court clerks see cases at the very beginning—from filing to trial to judgment. Given the often time sensitive nature of most proceedings, district court clerks work under tight deadlines to research how the judge should rule on motions, objections, or jury instructions. Because federal district court clerks assist judges in making critical trial-related decisions that may ultimately be reviewed on appeal by the federal appellate courts, clerks researching and advising their judges often look to how appellate courts review a particular question. Where appellate clerks may attend oral argument every six weeks, district court clerks can spend six weeks observing a single trial. In short, the pace is faster at district court.

Federal district court clerkships are also less isolating than appellate clerkships. In addition to interacting with their judge, the judge's judicial assistant, and a co-clerk (most district court judges just have two clerks), federal district court clerks interact with lawyers, witnesses, parties, court reporters, probation officers, deputy court clerks, bailiffs, and other court staff.[20] And, since federal district judges have their chambers in a court building, clerks will often get to know the other trial judges, magistrate judges, and clerks in the building.

Who should clerk at the federal district level? Graduates who want a federal litigation practice will certainly benefit from a federal district court clerkship. And while these clerkships are marketable nationwide, they are especially beneficial in the jurisdiction where you want to practice since you will learn the local court rules and various judges' preferences. Additionally, graduates

---

[20] Kate Bally, *10 Things To Know About Clerking In The Federal District*, ABOVE THE LAW (Oct. 17, 2017, 5:31 PM), https://abovethelaw.com/2017/10/10-things-to-know-about-clerking-in-the-federal-district/.

who want an appellate practice can greatly benefit from having a district court clerkship. This is because federal appellate courts review errors committed at the district court level. As a federal district court clerk you can see how those errors happen and understand the trial process and the rules that govern the trial courts—information that will be valuable while working on appellate matters.

What qualifications do you need to clerk at the federal district court level? Just like with federal appellate clerkships, it depends. Generally, federal district court clerkships are not considered as competitive as federal appellate clerkships. This might be, in part, because there are more federal district court judges than federal appellate court judges. There are currently 677 active federal district court judges spread across 94 judicial districts, which includes courts in several U.S. territories.[21] If each district court judge hires two clerks, approximately 1,354 clerkships are available each year or two. Plus, senior district court judges also handle cases and can hire term clerks.[22] Because these positions are not as competitive, you might not need to be as highly ranked in your law school class to secure a federal district court clerkship. This doesn't mean that your ranking is unimportant; it certainly is important, especially if you graduated from a lower ranked law school. But some federal district court judges may consider a wider swath of candidates than their friends on the appellate bench.

When should you apply for federal district court clerkships? Generally, the hiring timeline for these clerkships is the same as for federal appellate clerkships, which I discuss above.

---

[21] *List of Current United States District Judges*, WIKIPEDIA, https://en.wikipedia.org/wiki/List_of_current_United_States_district_judges (last visited July 20, 2022).

[22] *Id.*

One more point on federal district court clerkships. While most federal appellate clerkships are just one year (although some are two), it is common for federal district court judges to hire clerks for two-year terms. And district judges may also stagger their clerks so each new clerk overlaps with a senior clerk (for example, starting a new one-year clerk every February and every August). Finally, some firms offer the same clerkship signing bonus regardless of whether associates clerked at the federal appellate or trial level.[23]

Don't Forget the Federal Magistrates!

> *A law clerk may be tasked with opening and screening the judge's professional and personal correspondence, collaborating on law review articles and continuing legal education programs, and supervising judicial interns. He or she may serve as a frequent lunch companion, basketball teammate, and tennis or debate sparring partner, depending on specific chambers. It is not unusual for a law clerk, or former law clerk, to become a close and trusted friend of the judge.*
>
> ~Magistrate Judge Willie J. Epps[24]

Federal magistrate judges are an often-forgotten source of federal clerkships. When students tell me that they have been applying to *lots* of federal district court clerkships, I always ask if they have also applied to the magistrate judges. I am usually met with blank stares.

Federal magistrate judges are non-Article III judges, meaning they are not appointed and confirmed to their positions under

---

[23] Rubino, *supra* note 17.

[24] Willie J. Epps Jr. & Jonathan M. Warren, *The Who, What, When, Where, Why, and How of Clerking, as Told by a Federal Judge and His Former Law Clerk*, 90 UMKC L. REV. 295, 296 (2021).

Article III of the U.S. Constitution.[25] Rather, they are selected on a merit-based system in each of the 94 federal districts.[26] Magistrate judges serve renewable eight-year terms[27] and can have anywhere from zero to two term clerks depending on whether they have career clerks or a judicial assistant.

The work of magistrate judges, and thus their clerks, varies by district. In general, magistrate judges, and their clerks, do much of the same work that federal district court judges, and their clerks, do—researching, writing, conducting hearings, overseeing court matters, and performing administrative tasks (especially if the magistrate judge does not have a judicial assistant). For example, in criminal cases, a federal magistrate judge may:

- conduct initial appearances and arraignments for defendants accused of felony offenses,

- appoint counsel for criminal defendants,

- determine whether criminal defendants will be detained or released on a bond,

- assess whether a case merits dismissal,

- take guilty pleas in felony cases,

- issue search and arrest warrants, and

- assess petitions for habeas corpus.[28]

In civil cases magistrates can hear an entire matter if both parties consent.[29] They can also do the following:

---

[25]   Fed. Mag. JJ. Ass'n, *What is a Federal Magistrate Judge?*, FMJA, at 1 (2021), *available at* https://fmja.org/wp-content/uploads/2021/07/What-is-a-Magistrate-Judge-for-FJMA-webpage.pdf.

[26]   *Id.*

[27]   *Id.* at 2.

[28]   *Id.* I take slight umbrage with this list because habeas corpus cases are technically civil, although they typically arise from what was originally a criminal matter.

[29]   *Id.* at 3.

- make final determinations on a wide variety of preliminary and non-dispositive motions,

- make determinations of fact,

- make recommendations to the district judge on dispositive motions such a[s] summary judgment,

- conduct mediations,

- resolve discovery and other pretrial disputes, and

- recommend whether a Social Security claimant should receive a disability award.[30]

As you can see from these lists, clerking for a magistrate judge is a great way to get hands-on experience in federal district court. Observing and assisting in resolving discovery disputes is particularly valuable experience, as many litigation matters turn on what evidence is admissible at summary judgment and trial. Furthermore, federal magistrate judges are sometimes selected for federal district court or federal appellate court positions, so what starts as a magistrate clerkship could morph into something else.[31]

The qualifications to clerk for a magistrate judge are similar to those of federal district court clerks, but perhaps slightly less competitive, in part because many students don't know to apply to magistrate judges. There are approximately 549 full-time magistrate judges,[32] so clerk openings abound across the judicial districts.

When and how do you apply for federal magistrate judge clerkships? Some magistrate judges, like other federal judges, follow the federal law clerk hiring plan. For those judges, the

---

[30]   *Id.*

[31]   *Id.* at 2.

[32]   *Id.*

timeline I discuss under federal appellate judges would apply.[33] Chances are, however, that you might not know if magistrate judges follow the federal hiring plan timeline. Therefore, it behooves career services offices to connect with "local" federal magistrate judges to ascertain their hiring needs and schedules. I put "local" in air quotes because it should be defined quite broadly. For example, career services offices should check with the chambers of federal magistrate judges in the entire state and neighboring states from which that school attracts a large number of students. If your career services office doesn't have that information (or isn't willing to check for you and get it), you as an applicant need to call each magistrate's chambers and ask about hiring preferences and timelines. Chambers personnel receive these calls often and are typically very willing to share timing information.

State Appellate Court

> *If you plan to practice criminal law, my court is an excellent place to work. Since we are the Court of last resort on criminal matters, clerks gain a wide variety of knowledge and experience. Knowing how the ultimate court "thinks" is always beneficial. Clerks can learn the basic, but important, research and writing skills that may be a step beyond what they learn in law school; in turn, the can use that knowledge as it applies to their future practice.*

~Judge Barbara Parker Hervey[34]

State appellate court clerkships generally fall into two categories—state intermediate appellate court and state supreme court positions. I use the term "state supreme court" to refer to the

---

[33] Unless, of course, the federal hiring plan is defunct when you are reading this book.

[34] JUDICIAL CLERKSHIP FORUM, *supra* note 8, at 10.

highest level of state court—the court of last resort. Nearly every state, except New York, designates its highest court as a "supreme court." In New York, however, the highest court is the New York Court of Appeals.[35] Some states, like Texas, have separate courts of last resort for civil and criminal matters.[36] Not every state appellate court accepts term clerks. Some courts, like the California Supreme Court, do not hire term clerks.[37]

As I discussed in Chapter 1, many of the top law schools focus on federal appellate clerkships to the detriment of state appellate clerkships. But, state appellate clerkships offer most of the same experiential benefits as federal appellate clerkships. Clerks at state appellate courts, like their federal counterparts, do a significant amount of research and writing on cases before the court. While their work varies by court, in general, clerks prepare bench memoranda on cases, help prepare judges for oral argument, and write draft opinions in cases. Some state appellate courts, like the Georgia Supreme Court, hear a lot of oral argument.[38] Other courts, like the Oklahoma Supreme Court, rarely hear oral arguments and decide cases on the filings and the record.[39] If observing oral argument is important to you, you will want to investigate how often the state appellate court you are applying to hears oral argument. That information can usually be found on the state court website.

---

[35] *Court Structure*, N.Y. STATE UNIFIED CT. SYS., https://ww2.nycourts.gov/courts/8jd/structure.shtml (last visited July 20, 2022).

[36] *Texas Courts: A Descriptive Summary*, TEX. JUD. BRANCH 2, *available at* https://www.txcourts.gov/media/994672/Court-Overview.pdf.

[37] Vt. Pub. Int. Action Project Office of Career Servs., *The 2021-2022 Guide to State Court Judicial Clerkship Procedures*, VT. LAW SCH. at 17 (2021), *available at* https://cpb-us-w2.wpmucdn.com/sites.northeastern.edu/dist/b/232/files/2020/08/Vermont-Guide-to-State-Clerk-Courtships-2021-22.pdf (hereinafter "Vermont Guide").

[38] *See, e.g.*, *Oral Arguments*, SUP. CT. OF GA., https://www.gasupreme.us/watch/ (last visited July 20, 2022).

[39] *The Supreme Court*, OKLA. STATE CTS. NETWORK, https://www.oscn.net/schome/ (last visited July 20, 2022).

Clerking at the state appellate level also offers many of the same career benefits as clerking in federal court, minus the huge signing bonuses (sorry). Like federal appellate clerkships, state appellate clerkships allow you to build a close working relationship with a judge who may become a lifelong mentor. You will also learn how the court operates and the preferences of the judges, something that will be extremely valuable to law firms with state appellate practices. And, while state appellate clerkships may not carry the same cachet as federal appellate clerkships among *some* lawyers (you know I am talking about graduates from highly ranked law schools), most other lawyers (and your grandparents) will find the credential quite impressive. A clerkship is a clerkship!

What qualifications do you need to clerk at the state appellate level? Generally, like with federal appellate clerkships, it is important to demonstrate strong research and writing skills. You should get good grades in writing classes, work on a law journal, and secure strong letters of recommendation. While students who graduate near the top of their class are likely to be more competitive in the application process, especially at the state supreme court level, I have seen students in the top 30% of their class secure state supreme court clerkships. Furthermore, it is less important to have graduated from a top-ten law school for state appellate clerkships. State appellate judges, who are often themselves graduates of the law schools in that state, prize applications from the law schools in that state, especially their alma mater, or from law students with connections to the state who intend to practice there.

How prestigious are state appellate clerkships? Well, it depends. As I mentioned above, if you want to have a state appellate practice, then a state appellate clerkship in that state is highly valuable. In fact, I would argue that it is more practical than a federal clerkship. If you plan on practicing in a different state, a state appellate court clerkship might not be as valued as a federal clerkship, but I think that most legal employers would still appreciate the intense writing and researching skills that you honed during your clerkship year.

When do you apply for state appellate clerkships? If your guess is, "it depends" you would be right. My research assistants and I did a state survey to try and answer this question. We found that most state appellate courts hire in the spring of the 2L year or the summer immediately following the 2L year. A few state appellate courts hire in fall of the 2L year, a few in the 3L year, and in a few others it varies by judge. Just like with the magistrate judges, career services offices need to know the hiring practices in state appellate courts. In fact, a few law schools have tried to compile these resources, but any resource can be quickly outdated as practices (and judges) change.[40] When in doubt about timelines, a phone call to the clerk's office or to a judge's chambers can clear up any uncertainty.

State Trial Court

> My first job out of law school was as a law clerk in Adams County District Court, and I loved it! . . . I loved the incredible exposure I received at the district court job to the legal system and procedures, seeing different types of cases, meeting judges and lawyers, working with staff, and interacting with the public.
>
> ~Judge Mariana Vielma[41]

---

[40]   *See* Vermont Guide, *supra* note 37.

[41]   Mallory A. Revel, *A Conversation with Judge Mariana Vielma*, 50 Colo. Law. 50, 51 (2021).

If you want to be a prosecutor, public defender, or litigator in state court, then clerking for a state trial court judge is an excellent opportunity to get experience.

Not all state trial courts have term clerk positions, and in some state trial courts, multiple judges share a single term clerk, meaning that the clerk probably spends more time researching and writing and less time watching court proceedings. But, for the jurisdictions where a clerk is assigned to a specific judge, clerking in state trial court will provide you with a firsthand look at what works at trial and what doesn't. It will probably also offer you a lifetime supply of amusing stories to share at cocktail parties.[42]

The duties of state trial court clerks vary by jurisdiction and bench (or type of court). For example, if you clerk for a judge with a civil bench, you might be in court less and spend more time researching and writing. But, if you clerk for a judge on a criminal, family, or juvenile bench, you will likely spend significant time assisting the judge and other court staff with managing the judge's docket and courtroom. Either way, after a one-year or two-year clerkship you will know what judges like to see in court, which attorneys are effective and well-respected by the court, and what arguments persuade juries. This information is incredibly valuable to firms and government agencies that regularly practice in state trial court.

What are the qualifications for clerking at the state trial level? From what I have seen in Arizona, grades, class rank, and journal service are less important. Judges do want to know that you can research and write, but being able to manage people—like juries, attorneys, and witnesses—is also important. Judges might also like

---

[42]   But remember as a clerk you owe your judge a duty of confidentiality. So, your cocktail parties stories need to be about the crazy things you observed in public court proceedings—like the person charged with a drug offense wearing to court a t-shirt that promotes drug use—and not about the things you and your judge discuss. See Chapter 6 for a more detailed discussion of your ethical responsibilities as a clerk.

to see internships with a prosecutor or public defender office and a good grasp of the rules of evidence.

When and how do you apply? Well, it depends on the state and court. In Arizona, our state court trial judges hire clerks during a student's 3L year. In other states, however, this hiring is done in the 2L year.[43] Some judges and jurisdictions have a formal application process, and other judges seek applicants when they have openings. You should check with your career services office for information about your jurisdiction, call the clerk's office to ask, or reach out to specific judges for more information about their clerkships.

One final word about state trial clerkships—be sure to consider the expected salary and whether it works for you. In Arizona, for example, our state trial court clerks are not paid well. That isn't true in other states. Despite this low pay, I still think state trial clerkships are extremely valuable for students who want to regularly practice in state trial court. In fact, the valuable experience you gain clerking at state trial court could result in a higher salary post-clerkship.

Administrative Court

> [T]housands of people come before the administrative law courts and it is one of the few times that most citizens experience a hearing, as there are so many different areas that affect and impact their lives. . . . Oftentimes, the litigants are unrepresented by attorneys and have no public defender.
>
> ~Judge Bruce Cooper[44]

---

[43]   Vermont Guide, *supra* note 37.

[44]   Judge Cooper is a state administrative law judge. JUDICIAL CLERKSHIP FORUM, *supra* note 8, at 12.

In the federal court system, federal appellate and federal district court judges are referred to as Article III judges, meaning that their positions are subject to Article III of the Constitution. They are nominated by the President and confirmed by the Senate. They also have life tenure. There are other judges in the federal system, however, who are not subject to Article III. I have already discussed one group of non-Article III judges who offer clerkships— magistrate judges. Federal administrative law judges (ALJs) are another source of non-Article III clerkships. If you want to work in a field that is regulated by a federal or state agency, then clerking for an ALJ within that agency is a great opportunity to learn how that agency operates.[45]

Numerous federal administrative agencies have ALJs, but not all these judges have term clerks. Some federal ALJs hire term clerks through the DOJ Honors Program—the Drug Enforcement Administration and the Executive Office for Immigration Review.[46] The DOJ Honors program is "the nation's premier entry-level federal attorney recruitment program."[47] In general, it is open to students who just graduated from law school or recent graduates who clerked or completed a legal fellowship immediately after law school.[48] Applications for these clerkships are currently due near the start of the 3L year. Other ALJs hire on a more ad hoc basis. Many of these jobs are posted on usajobs.gov. You can also mail applications directly to the various ALJ offices. The National Association for Law Placement (NALP) offers an excellent guide on federal ALJ

---

[45] *2021-2022 Judicial Clerkships Handbook*, Richmond Sch. of Law 5, https://law.richmond.edu/career/_pdf/Clerkship-Handbook.pdf (last visited July 20, 2022).

[46] *Honors Program Participating Components*, U.S. Dep't of Just., https://www.justice.gov/legal-careers/honors-program-participating-components   (last visited July 20, 2022).

[47] *The Attorney General's Honors Program*, U.S. Dep't of Just., https://www.justice.gov/legal-careers/entry-level-attorneys (last visited August 5, 2022).

[48] *Id.*

clerkships that should serve as a starting point for graduates interested in these opportunities.[49]

What do ALJ clerks do? Like most clerks they research matters before the ALJ and write memoranda and orders. ALJ clerks also assist ALJs with hearings, much like federal district court clerks assist judges with hearings and trials. These hearings may include evidentiary hearings or settlement conferences, and they generally follow the procedures set forth in the Administrative Procedures Act. The exact duties of clerks will depend on the agency, but let me give you a few examples of what the specific administrative courts do, which will give you a taste for what the clerks do. If the subject matter of the agency interests you, or you think that you will ultimately practice in an area that falls under that agency's jurisdiction, then you should consider clerking for an ALJ at that agency.

- **Drug Enforcement Administration (DEA).** These ALJs hear matters brought by the Drug Enforcement Agency under the Controlled Substances Act. They may also hear cases from the Federal Bureau of Prisons and the Bureau of Alcohol, Tobacco, Firearms, and Explosives.[50]

- **Executive Office for Immigration Review (EOIR).** There are two potential administrative clerkship opportunities at EOIR. First, the Office of the Chief Immigration Judge hires 50 clerks through the Honors

---

[49]   *Federal Administrative Law Judges' Post Graduate Clerkship Hiring Information*, TEX. A&M SCH. OF LAW (2016), https://law.tamu.edu/docs/default-source/career-services-documents/federal_alj_post_graduate_clerkship_hiring_information.pdf?sfvrsn=2.

[50]   *Office of Administrative Law Judges*, U.S. DRUG ENF'T ADMIN., https://www.dea.gov/administrative-law-judges (last visited July 20, 2022).

program to assist Immigration Courts nationwide.[51] These courts adjudicate immigration cases, deciding questions like whether persons can remain in the U.S., whether asylum should be granted, and whether a person should be granted relief from deportation.[52] Clerkships are also available with the Board of Immigration Appeals (BIA), which hears appeals from lower immigration courts.[53] These BIA cases are largely decided on the filings, and this court rarely hears oral argument.[54] Students interested in immigration law would value from either of these opportunities.

- **United States Nuclear Regulatory Commission's Atomic Safety and Licensing Board Panel.** This Panel holds hearings on issues related to the licensing of nuclear reactors and "the construction of uranium enrichment facilities."[55] Its ALJ panels consist of both lawyers and experts in science or technical fields. Clerks assist the panel in preparing for hearings, "manage documentary materials for the adjudicatory record," and serve as a point of contact for the parties.[56]

---

[51] *Honors Program Participating Components*, U.S. DEP'T OF JUST., https://www.justice.gov/legal-careers/honors-program-participating-components (last visited July 20, 2022).

[52] *Immigration Court Primer*, TRAC IMMIGR., https://trac.syr.edu/immigration/quickfacts/about_eoir.html (last visited July 20, 2022).

[53] *Board of Immigration Appeals*, U.S. DEP'T OF JUST., https://www.justice.gov/eoir/board-of-immigration-appeals (last visited July 20, 2022).

[54] *Id.*

[55] *ASLBP Responsibilities*, U.S. NUCLEAR REGUL. COMM'N, https://www.nrc.gov/about-nrc/regulatory/adjudicatory/aslbp-respons.html (last visited July 20, 2022).

[56] *Judicial Law Clerk Program*, U.S. NUCLEAR REGUL. COMM'N, https://www.nrc.gov/about-nrc/employment/judicial-law-clerk.html (last visited July 20, 2022).

- **Environmental Protection Agency (EPA).** The EPA's ALJs "conduct hearings and render decisions in proceedings between EPA and persons, businesses, government entities, and other organizations that are, or are alleged to be, regulated under environmental laws."[57] For graduates interested in practicing environmental law, a clerkship with the EPA's ALJs would provide a firsthand look at the significant regulatory framework in this field of law.

- **Department of Labor (DOL).** DOL houses the third largest federal ALJ office, with ALJs in nine offices nationwide.[58] DOL ALJs hear a wide variety of matters, including cases where workers seek benefits under certain acts, like the Black Lung Benefits Act.[59] They also hear cases like "whistleblower complaints involving corporate fraud and violations of transportation, environmental and food safety statutes; . . . actions involving the working conditions of migrant farm laborers; . . . prohibition of workplace discrimination by government contractors; . . . federal contract disputes; . . . and standards of conduct in union elections." This would be an excellent clerkship for students interested in employment law or white collar defense work.

- **Federal Energy Regulatory Commission (FERC).** FERC "is an independent agency that regulates the interstate transmission of electricity, natural gas,

---

[57] *Filings, Procedures, Orders and Decisions of EPA's Administrative Law Judges*, U.S. ENV'T PROT. AGENCY, https://www.epa.gov/alj (last visited July 20, 2022).

[58] *About the Office of Administrative Law Judges*, U.S. DEP'T OF LAB., https://www.dol.gov/agencies/oalj/about/ALJMISSN (last visited July 20, 2022).

[59] *Id.*

and oil."[60] It also "reviews proposals to build . . . interstate natural gas pipelines, as well as licensing hydropower projects."[61] FERC ALJs handle contested cases in these matters. FERC has an organized clerkship program, with applications due at the start of the 3L year.[62] This would be an excellent clerkship for students interested in energy law.

What are the qualifications for clerking for a federal ALJ? Generally, the DOJ Honors program is quite competitive, and only a handful of spots are available each year. That said, I have seen strong candidates (meaning near the top of their class) from unranked law schools receive DOJ Honors spots. For ALJ clerkships that do not fall under DOJ Honors, it certainly helps to have an interest in the court's subject matter, in particular, and administrative law in general. Apart from that, the clerkship program for the United States Nuclear Regulatory Commission requires at least a 3.25 GPA.[63] Because many of these programs are not as well-known as federal or state court clerkships, I suspect that they are not as competitive and ALJs would prize subject matter interest over your class rank or the rank of your law school.

States also have administrative agencies with ALJs that hear cases. If you are interested in state administrative law, it would be worthwhile to contact your state agencies to see if the ALJs offer clerkship opportunities.

---

[60] *Legal Internships and ALJ Clerkships in OALJ*, FED. ENERGY REGUL. COMM'N, https://www.ferc.gov/legal-internships-and-alj-clerkships-oalj (last visited July 20,2022).

[61] *Id.*

[62] *Id.*

[63] *Judicial Law Clerk Program*, U.S. NUCLEAR REGUL. COMM'N, https://www.nrc.gov/about-nrc/employment/judicial-law-clerk.html (last visited July 20, 2022).

Specialty Courts

> The most challenging aspect of clerking on the US Court
> of International Trade is the complexity of the work,
> much of which is fiercely contested, high-stakes, "bet-
> the-farm" litigation. And, of course, every case is
> international in scope. It is not unusual for a case to
> involve three or more parties, and six or more distinct
> issues.

~Judge Delissa A. Ridgway[64]

Several other federal specialty courts also offer judicial
clerkships. These courts are less well-known, and thus clerkships are
less competitive. But, like with administrative law clerkships, ideal
candidates to federal specialty courts have an interest in practicing
in that particular field. This list certainly isn't exhaustive, but it
does touch on the most prominent specialty courts.

United States Court of Appeals for the Armed Forces

The Court of the Appeals for the Armed Forces (CAAF) hears
criminal appeals from four intermediate appellate courts connected
to the various service branches.[65] Decisions from CAAF are subject
to review by the U.S. Supreme Court through a petition for a writ of
certiorari. The CAAF is composed of five judges who typically sit as
a panel on all cases.[66] The judges post clerkship information,
including any required qualifications, on the court's website.[67]
Currently, the judges appear to be hiring clerks during the 2L

---

[64] Darhiana Mateo Tellez, *Clerkship Confidential*, 43 STUDENT LAW. 28, 36
(2015).

[65] *Judge Gregory E. Maggs*, U.S. CT. OF APPEALS FOR THE ARMED FORCES, https://
www.armfor.uscourts.gov/employment/maggs.htm (last visited July 20, 2022).

[66] *Judges*, U.S. CT. OF APPEALS FOR THE ARMED FORCES, https://www.armfor.
uscourts.gov/judges.htm (last visited July 20, 2022).

[67] *Employment*, U.S. CT. OF APPEALS FOR THE ARMED FORCES, https://www.armfor.
uscourts.gov/employment.htm (last visited July 20, 2022).

summer or at the start of the 3L year. One judge requires journal service and prefers students in the top 20% of their class,[68] while another seeks "top law school performers with strong research and legal writing skills."[69] None of the current judges require prior military service or knowledge of military law, although one of the judges notes that candidates interested in criminal law, appellate litigation, or becoming military attorneys would find the clerkship "especially interesting."[70]

If you are interested in military law, there are other military related courts that offer clerkships, including the United States Court of Appeals for Veterans Claims.[71]

United States Court of International Trade

The Court of International Trade, which is an Article III court, is composed of nine judges and acts as a trial court, with most matters being heard by a single judge, with a right of appeal to the Federal Circuit.[72] The court has jurisdiction over "civil actions arising out of import transactions and federal transactions affecting international trade."[73] Clerks with the Court of International Trade perform legal research, draft bench memos, and write opinions and

---

[68] *The Honorable Liam P. Hardy*, U.S. CT. OF APPEALS FOR THE ARMED FORCES, https://www.armfor.uscourts.gov/employment/hardy.htm (last visited July 20, 2022).

[69] *The Honorable Kevin A. Ohlson*, U.S. CT. OF APPEALS FOR THE ARMED FORCES, https://www.armfor.uscourts.gov/employment/ohlson.htm (last visited July 20, 2022).

[70] *Judge Gregory E. Maggs*, U.S. CT. OF APPEALS FOR THE ARMED FORCES, https://www.armfor.uscourts.gov/employment/maggs.htm (last visited July 20, 2022).

[71] *See, e.g., U.S. Court of Appeals for Veteran Claims*, USCAVC, http://m.uscourts.cavc.gov/ (last visited July 20, 2022).

[72] *About the Court*, U.S. CT. OF INT'L TRADE, https://www.cit.uscourts.gov/about-court (last visited July 20, 2022).

[73] *Id.*

orders.[74] Positions are listed on OSCAR, including specific qualifications for each judge.[75]

United States Court of Federal Claims

The Court of Federal Claims is a trial court that hears cases against the federal government where the claimants are seeking money.[76] Among the types of cases are pay claims, vaccine injury claims, tax claims, and patent and copyright claims.[77] Cases are appealed from the Court of Federal Claims to the Federal Circuit.[78] Currently, judges who are hiring list clerkship information on their biographical page.[79] The timing for applications appears to be quite diverse—from six months before clerkship start date to three years in advance![80]

United States Tax Court

The United States Tax Court hears taxpayer claims contesting IRS determinations.[81] It acts as a trial court, with appeals of right to the various federal appellate courts.[82] Many of the judges for the

---

[74] *Employment Opportunities*, U.S. CT. OF INT'L TRADE, https://www.cit. uscourts.gov/employment-opportunities (last visited July 20, 2022).

[75] *Id.*

[76] *Frequently Asked Questions*, U.S. CT. OF FED. CLAIMS, https://www.uscfc. uscourts.gov/faqs (last visited July 20, 2022).

[77] *Id.*

[78] *Id.*

[79] *Judges—Biographies*, U.S. CT. OF FED. CLAIMS, https://www.uscfc. uscourts.gov/judicial-officers (last visited July 20, 2022). *See, e.g., Judge Tapp's Employment Information*, U.S. CT. OF FED. CLAIMS, https://www.uscfc.uscourts. gov/judge-tapp-employment (last visited July 20, 2022); *Judge Holte's Employment Information*, U.S. CT. OF FED. CLAIMS, https://www.uscfc.uscourts.gov/judge-holte-employment (last visited July 20, 2022).

[80] *See, e.g., Judge Tapp's Employment Information*, U.S. CT. OF FED. CLAIMS, https://www.uscfc.uscourts.gov/judge-tapp-employment (last visited July 20, 2022); *Judge Holte's Employment Information*, U.S. CT. OF FED. CLAIMS, https://www.uscfc. uscourts.gov/judge-holte-employment (last visited July 20, 2022).

[81] *History*, U.S. TAX CT., https://www.ustaxcourt.gov/history.html (last visited July 20, 2022).

[82] *Guide for Petitioners: Things that Occur After Trial*, U.S. TAX CT., https:// www.ustaxcourt.gov/petitioners_after.html (last visited July 20, 2022).

Tax Court hire at a fall "Law Clerk Interview Day."[83] Unlike some of the other federal specialty courts, the Tax Court Judges prefer, and sometimes require, extensive knowledge of tax law and even some prior practice experience or an LLM in taxation.[84] Judges also prefer candidates with law review experience who graduate in the top third of their class.[85] The current openings, application process, and specific requirements for the judges who are hiring are listed on a separate webpage.[86]

Bankruptcy Court

Bankruptcy judges, like magistrate judges, are another forgotten source of clerkships. While bankruptcy courts are specialized courts, a wide variety of issues can be present in bankruptcy cases, including contract disputes, family law, intellectual property matters, tax law, employment law, environmental law, and real estate.[87] Thus, bankruptcy court clerkships are an excellent opportunity for students looking for a fast-paced trial-level clerkship.[88] And, most judges don't even require you to take a bankruptcy class in law school.[89] And lest you think that a bankruptcy clerkship will force you into a bankruptcy

---

[83]   *Law Clerk Program*, U.S. TAX CT., https://www.ustaxcourt.gov/law_clerk_program.html (last visited July 20, 2022).

[84]   *Id.*

[85]   *Id.*

[86]   *Judges Currently Recruiting*, U.S. TAX CT., https://www.ustaxcourt.gov/judges_recruiting.html (last visited July 20, 2022).

[87]   *Top 10 Reasons to be a U.S. Bankruptcy Court Clerk/Extern/Intern*, NAT'L CONF. OF BANKR. JJ., https://cdn.ymaws.com/www.ncbj.org/resource/resmgr/docs_public/NCBJ_Top_10_Reasons_to_Be_a_.pdf (last visited July 20, 2022); CCD Staff, *Quick Bankruptcy Q&A by Prof. D'Onfro*, WASH. UNIV. SCH. OF LAW (June 25, 2018), https://sites.law.wustl.edu/WashULaw/CCD_Blog/quick-bankruptcy-q-a-by-prof-donfro/.

[88]   *Top 10 Reasons to be a U.S. Bankruptcy Court Clerk/Extern/Intern*, NAT'L CONF. OF BANKR. JJ., https://cdn.ymaws.com/www.ncbj.org/resource/resmgr/docs_public/NCBJ_Top_10_Reasons_to_Be_a_.pdf (last visited July 20, 2022).

[89]   *Is a Bankruptcy Court Clerkship Right for You?*, CORNELL LAW SCH., https://community.lawschool.cornell.edu/careers/judicial-clerkships/clerkship-advice/is-a-bankruptcy-court-clerkship-right-for-you/ (last visited July 20, 2022). *See also* JUDICIAL CLERKSHIP FORUM, *supra* note 8, at 25.

career, while some bankruptcy court clerks go on to practice bankruptcy law, others "go on to general civil litigation work, commercial litigation practice, or transactional careers with firms of all sizes."[90]

There are 90 bankruptcy courts in the United States and a total of 347 authorized judgeships.[91] Like with magistrate judge clerkships, you can apply for these clerkships either through OSCAR or by contacting the individual chambers. Career services offices should be familiar with the hiring practices of the local bankruptcy judges.

Federal Circuit

The Federal Circuit is an appellate court with specific jurisdiction over certain types of cases, including patent, trademark, international trade, veterans' benefits, and some monetary claims against the United States. As noted above, several of the federal specialty trial courts offer a right of appeal to the Federal Circuit. While hiring on the Federal Circuit is competitive, it is generally less competitive than the other federal appellate courts. Additionally, some judges prefer candidates with experience, interest, or coursework in the areas that fall under the Federal Circuit's jurisdiction, like patent or trademark law. For graduates who want to practice in the areas that fall under the Federal Circuit's jurisdiction, a Federal Circuit clerkship is especially valuable. But even if you don't want to be a patent

---

[90] *Id.*

[91] *U.S. Bankruptcy Courts—Judicial Business 2018*, U.S. CTS., https:// www.uscourts.gov/statistics-reports/us-bankruptcy-courts-judicial-business-2018#:~: text=The%20federal%20Judiciary%20has%2090,Western%20DistrictsöfÄrkansas%20 https://www.uscourts.gov/statistics-reports/us-bankruptcy-courts-judicial-business-2018 (last visited July 20, 2022); *Status of Bankruptcy Judgeships—Judicial Business 2019*, U.S. CTS., https://www.uscourts.gov/statistics-reports/status-bankruptcy-judgeships-judicial-business-2019 (last visited July 20, 2022).

lawyer, clerking at the Federal Circuit will give you insight into appellate practice and appellate decision-making.

In terms of the how and when to apply, the judges on the Federal Circuit currently hire using OSCAR and the federal clerkship hiring plan.

Delaware Court of Chancery

There is one additional specialty court that deserves mention— the Delaware Court of Chancery. For graduates who want to practice corporate law, clerking at the Delaware Court of Chancery is akin to a SCOTUS clerkship. Why? Because many corporations are incorporated in Delaware, and the Court of Chancery has jurisdiction to hear civil cases involving these corporations.

The Court of Chancery is a non-jury trial court that operates at a fast pace, so clerks "are able to see many cases go through the entire lifecycle from complaint to final resolution."[92] Like other trial court clerks, Court of Chancery clerks research law, help prepare opinions, and attend arguments and trials.[93]

These clerkships are considered highly selective, with one clerkship guide saying that they are "on par with competitive federal circuit court positions."[94] According to the court's website, applications are accepted in the fall of the 2L year.[95]

---

[92]   *Clerkships at the Delaware Court of Chancery*, DEL. CT. OF CHANCERY, https://courts.delaware.gov/chancery/clerkship/ (last visited July 20, 2022).

[93]   *Id.*

[94]   *Judicial Clerkship Manual*, GEORGETOWN LAW (2020), https://www.law.georgetown.edu/wp-content/uploads/2020/05/Judicial-Clerkships-Manual-20-01-15.pdf.

[95]   *Clerkships at the Delaware Court of Chancery*, DEL. CT. OF CHANCERY, https://courts.delaware.gov/chancery/clerkship/ (last visited July 20, 2022).

Tribal Court

The federal and state court systems are not the only court systems in the United States. There are also approximately 400 Tribal court systems in the United States as well as five regional Court of Indian Offenses (CFR) systems for Tribes that lack a court system.[96] For students who are interested in practicing in Tribal courts, or who are generally interested in Indian law, clerking for a Tribal court is a great option.

Unfortunately, like state court clerkships, Tribal court clerkship information is not collected in one central repository. Furthermore, some Tribal courts (again like some state courts) lack detailed websites. Thus, students who are interested in Tribal court clerkships need to proactively research Tribal courts and reach out to them for information about clerkships.[97] And, if the court doesn't offer a clerkship, it never hurts to ask if they would consider a pilot clerkship program. For example, the Yale Law School international clerkship guide tells the story of a student who was interested in clerking at the Supreme Court of India. When he reached out to the Chief Justice of that court, he found out that the court had never hired clerks. His contact with them, however, led the court to consider and ultimately implement a clerkship program.[98]

What do Tribal court clerks do? The work of Tribal court clerks will certainly vary by Tribe and by type of court—trial or appellate court. Generally, however, the work is likely to mirror the work of clerks in similar types of courts at the state level. For example, clerks at a Tribal supreme court will do significant research and

---

[96]　*Tribal Court Systems*, U.S. DEP'T OF INTERIOR, INDIAN AFFS., https://www.bia.gov/CFRCourts/tribal-justice-support-directorate (last visited July 20, 2022).

[97]　The Tribal Court Clearinghouse keeps a detailed list of Tribal courts that includes contact information where available. *Tribal Courts*, TRIBAL CT. CLEARINGHOUSE, http://www.tribal-institute.org/lists/justice.htm (last visited July 20, 2022).

[98]　*Opportunities with International Tribunals and Foreign Courts*, YALE LAW SCH. CAREER DEV. OFF. 4 (2018), https://law.yale.edu/sites/default/files/area/department/cdo/document/cdo_international_tribunals_public.pdf.

writing work. But what makes the work of Tribal courts especially interesting is seeing how Tribal law and custom influences the court's work.[99]

What qualifications do you need to clerk at the Tribal court level? Some Tribal courts may have hiring preferences for Tribal members. Tribal courts may also require knowledge of Tribal law or Indigenous languages.[100] In addition to these specialized skills, strong research and writing skills are always a plus.

Foreign, International, or Intergovernmental Court

This experience opened my eyes to the procedural processes of the EU's Court of Justice (which are quite different from those of U.S. courts) and substantive European law. It also provided a window into how 27 diverse member-states can come together and work through (and benefit from) differences in culture, language, and legal tradition for the common goal of ensuring the integrity of EU law.[101]

~Carolyn Black

Judicial clerkships are not just limited to courts in the United States. Courts in other countries and various international or intergovernmental courts and tribunals offer clerkships.[102] These clerkships often look different from clerkships with courts inside the United States. For example, they might be for a shorter duration,

---

[99] For a look at the Navajo Supreme Court see JoAnn B. Jayne, *Duty of Fairness and Healing*, 21 J. APP. PRAC. & PROCESS 277 (2021).

[100] *See, e.g., The Judicial Branch of the Navajo Nation Job Vacancy Announcement*, NAVAJO NATION CTS. (June 6, 2022), http://www.courts.navajo-nsn.gov/HR/2022/Supreme%20Court%20Law%20Clerk%207.31.22.pdf.

[101] Craig Ferguson, *Experiencing a Clerkship at the European Court of Justice*, DIPNOTE (Jan. 31, 2022), https://www.state.gov/dipnote-u-s-department-of-state-official-blog/experiencing-a-clerkship-at-the-european-court-of-justice/.

[102] *Opportunities with International Tribunals and Foreign Courts*, YALE LAW SCH. CAREER DEV. OFF. (2018), https://law.yale.edu/sites/default/files/area/department/cdo/document/cdo_international_tribunals_public.pdf.

they might be unpaid, and they might also be open to current students, not just graduates.[103]

Why might a graduate want to clerk for a foreign, international, or intergovernmental court? For some graduates it might be because the court addresses a subject matter that interests them, such as international human rights, arbitration, or international criminal matters.[104] Others may have career plans that include international work, and an international clerkship would give them exposure to aspects of that work. And others may just want a unique clerkship experience.

Naturally, the qualifications for international or intergovernmental clerkships vary by clerkship. Some require foreign language proficiency. Some foreign national courts might also require other documentation if your law degree was obtained outside of that country.

Like with Tribal clerkships, foreign, international, or intergovernmental courts that do not offer clerkships may still be willing to consider a pilot clerkship program, so it never hurts to reach out to a jurisdiction or court where you might want to clerk. Yale Law School[105] and Columbia Law School[106] have useful guides to international clerkships that list some of the available positions. Examples of possible foreign, international, or intergovernmental clerkships include the:

---

[103] A great example of this is a clerkship at the Supreme Court of Israel. Clerkships with that court are unpaid, open to current law students, and last for three months. *Foreign Clerkships at the Supreme Court of Israel*, STATE OF ISR., JUD. AUTH. SUP. CT., https://supreme.court.gov.il/sites/en/Documents/Foreign%20Clerkships%20at%20the%20Supreme%20court.pdf (last visited July 20, 2022).

[104] *Opportunities with International Tribunals and Foreign Courts*, YALE LAW SCH. CAREER DEV. OFF. 4 (2018), https://law.yale.edu/sites/default/files/area/department/cdo/document/cdo_international_tribunals_public.pdf.

[105] *See id.*

[106] *International Clerkships*, COLUMBIA LAW SCH. (2018), https://clawstage.ohodev.com/sites/default/files/2020-01/international_clerkships_guide.100318.pdf.pdf.

- **Constitutional Court of South Africa,**[107] the highest court in South Africa.[108]

- **Court of Justice of the European Union,**[109] which is the legal arm of the European Union. Its duties include interpreting European Union law "to make sure it is applied in the same way in all EU countries, and settl[ing] legal disputes between national governments and EU institutions."[110]

- **European Court of Human Rights,**[111] which "rules on individual or State applications alleging violations of the civil and political rights set out in the European Convention on Human Rights."[112]

- **International Court of Justice,**[113] which "is the principal judicial organ of the United Nations."[114]

- **International Criminal Court,**[115] which "investigates and . . . tries individuals charged with the gravest

---

[107] *Constitutional Court of South Africa*, AM. SOC'Y OF INT'L LAW, https://www.asil.org/sites/default/files/ILPOST/pdfs/140206_South_African_Court.pdf   (last visited July 20, 2022).

[108] *Id.*

[109] *The 2022-2023 Dean Acheson Legal Stage Program*, CT. OF JUST. OF THE EUR. UNION,   https://uploads.mwp.mprod.getusinfo.com/uploads/sites/8/2022/02/dean-acheson-stage-flyer-2022-23-us-embassy-luxembourg_v2.pdf (last visited July 20, 2022).

[110] *Court of Justice of the European Union*, EUR. UNION, https://european-union.europa.eu/institutions-law-budget/institutions-and-bodies/institutions-and-bodies-profiles/court-justice-european-union-cjeu_en (last visited July 20, 2022) (emphasis removed).

[111] *Recruitment and Traineeships*, EUR. CT. OF HUM. RTS., https://www.echr.coe.int/Pages/home.aspx?p=employmentandtraineeships&c (last visited July 20, 2022).

[112] *The European Court of Human Rights*, COUNCIL OF EUR., https://www.coe.int/en/web/tbilisi/europeancourtofhumanrights (last visited July 20, 2022).

[113] *Judicial Fellowship Program*, INT'L CT. OF JUST., https://www.icj-cij.org/en/judicial-fellows-program (last visited July 20, 2022).

[114] *The Court*, INT'L CT. OF JUST., https://www.icj-cij.org/en/court (last visited July 20, 2022).

[115] *Jobs*, INT'L CRIM. CT., https://www.icc-cpi.int/jobs (last visited July 20, 2022).

crimes of concern to the international community: genocide, war crimes, crimes against humanity and the crime of aggression."[116]

- **European Free Trade Agreement Court,**[117] which "interpret[s] the Agreement on the European Economic Area with regard to the EFTA States party to the Agreement."[118]

- **Federal Court of Canada,**[119] which, among other things, "review[s] decisions of all federal boards, commissions, and tribunals."[120] It also has subject-matter jurisdiction in the follow areas: "Crown actions, immigration, citizenship, national security, indigenous peoples, human rights, admiralty, customs, intellectual property, tax, labour relations, transportation, communications, parole and corrections."[121]

- **Supreme Court of Israel,**[122] which is the highest court in Israel.[123]

---

[116] *About the Court*, INT'L CRIM. CT., https://www.icc-cpi.int/about/the-court (last visited July 20, 2022).

[117] *Trainees*, EFTA, https://eftacourt.int/the-court/trainees/ (last visited July 20, 2022).

[118] *The Court*, EFTA, https://eftacourt.int/the-court/ (last visited July 20, 2022).

[119] *Law Clerk Program*, FED. CT. OF CAN., https://www.fct-cf.gc.ca/en/pages/about-the-court/careers/law-clerk-program (last visited July 20, 2022).

[120] *History*, FED. CT. OF CAN., https://www.fct-cf.gc.ca/en/pages/about-the-court/history (last visited July 20, 2022).

[121] *Id.*

[122] *Foreign Clerkships at the Supreme Court*, ST. OF ISR., JUD. AUTH. SUP. CT. https://supreme.court.gov.il/sites/en/Pages/Staffing.aspx (last visited July 20, 2022).

[123] *About the Supreme Court*, ST. OF ISR., JUD. AUTH. SUP. CT. https://supreme.court.gov.il/sites/en/Pages/Overview.aspx (last visited July 20, 2022).

Summing It All up

As you can see from the discussion above, clerkships are more than just what is offered at the federal appellate level. A myriad of available clerkships address a wide swath of subject matters and jurisdictions. For graduates who know that they want to practice in a particular field—specialized courts or administrative agencies can offer valuable experience. For other students, more generalized courts can expose them to many different practice areas and attorney styles. And all of these clerkships can offer excellent mentoring and training from the judges who supervise clerk work.

Short & Happy!

- There are a wide variety of clerkships available.
- Don't forget about the non-Article III federal judges, like magistrates or administrative law judges.
- State courts often offer many clerkship opportunities, which are excellent training for graduates who want to practice in that state.

CHAPTER 3

WHY Should You Clerk?

[Clerking] spills out annually into the bar a batch of young lawyers—future leaders—who know from the inside that the appellate courts move with continuity, and move with responsibility, that they answer to their duty to the 'law,' that they move not as individuals or as persons, but as officers . . . .

~Karl Llewellyn[1]

If you have read everything in this book up to this point, you know I think judicial clerkships are a valuable experience. I would even go so far as to say that a clerkship is the best legal job out there for new or recent graduates. Why? In this chapter I will give you nine reasons why I think you should clerk.

Reason #1: It Gives You Another Year to Decide What You Want to Do with the Rest of Your Life

I refer to my clerks as my family constantly in emails, in conversation. And I don't mean it as a rhetorical trope. I

---

[1]   KARL LLEWELLYN, THE COMMON LAW TRADITION: DECIDING APPEALS 322 (1960).

mean as a genuine heartfelt feeling. For the year that we're together, we have this unbelievable bond because we get to work on things that other people don't get to see . . . .

~Judge Andrew Oldham[2]

A common misperception among law students is that everyone else in law school (except you of course) has their &*#! together. Guess what? They don't. If you feel insecure, out of place, and not at all sure what you want to do with the rest of your legal career, welcome to the club. And, even if you went to law school thinking you knew what you wanted to do with your legal career, there is nothing quite like the peer pressure of law school to make you rethink everything that you thought you wanted to do.

This is where clerking comes in—it gives you one or more years, removed from the pressure of law school, to figure out what you want to do with your life. And not only do you have extra time to figure it out, but during your clerkship year(s) you will be exposed to a wide variety of legal questions and attorneys. You can see what cases interest you and what kinds of attorneys you want to emulate. Furthermore, you will have a new mentor, your judge, and new friends, your co-clerks, who can provide a fresh perspective on your career.

If this reason for clerking appeals to you, I would recommend seeking a more "general" clerkship, like a state or federal appellate or trial clerkship. These clerkships are more likely to expose you to a greater variety of cases and subject matters.

---

[2] *Judgment Calls with Hon. David F. Levi*, Bolch Judicial Institute Duke Law (Jun. 11, 2021), https://judicialstudies.duke.edu/2021/06/s2-ep3-the-incredible-indescribable-clerkship/.

Reason #2: It Allows You to Make a Career Transition

There's a lot of practical value to you in seeing the way the courts work. You're seeing the inside of how the courts function. When you return to the outside, and you're practicing in front of the courts, you have a sense of what's going on in that decision-making process.

~Justice Amy Coney Barrett[3]

During law school, students are often pressured to find post-graduation jobs at big law firms. This pressure can come from fellow students, faculty, and even the career services office. As a student, it can be hard to turn down a law firm job after graduation—especially if you have student loans to repay and the firm starting salary is over $200k.

Many graduates, after following the siren's call of a law firm job, soon realize that big firm life isn't for them. Maybe they hate corporate transactional work. Maybe they hate New York City. Or maybe they just hate working a ridiculous number of hours each week. This is where a clerkship can come in. You can secure a state or federal appellate clerkship, rebrand yourself as an appellate attorney, and move to a new location with a slower-paced lifestyle.

Recent graduates coming to clerkships from practice have several advantages. First, you are not bound by the federal clerkship hiring plan, so you can sign up for OSCAR and apply at any time. Second, you are not waiting for a graduation date. You could be ready to clerk for a judge who is confirmed in the middle of an academic year. Third, you have experience. As I have already mentioned, more and more judges are preferring clerkship

---

[3] Kevin Allen, *Seventh Circuit judges share advice, insights on clerkships*, UNIVERSITY OF NOTRE DAME SCHOOL OF LAW (Feb. 5, 2020), https://law.nd.edu/news-events/news/seventh-circuit-judges-clerkships-panel/.

candidates with prior legal experience. In the federal system, this work experience will also give you a pay bump. It won't rival your Biglaw salary, but it is something.

You can use any type of clerkship to transition your career, assuming that particular clerkship is open to recent graduates, which most are.[4] You should just keep in mind the reasons for your transition—location or subject matter—and find a clerkship that furthers those reasons.

Reason #3: It Exposes You to Many Different Areas of the Law

> *I think clerking is interesting, particularly in intermediate court like mine where there is general appellate jurisdiction. It really gives an opportunity to see the wide array of issues that come across a lawyer's desk.*

~Judge Margret G. Robb[5]

You know what one of the best parts about being an attorney is? It's when your neighbor or a random airplane seatmate asks you, a professor, a legal question about their divorce, real estate matter, or contract dispute and expects you to know the answer.[6] In these situations I usually look at the person and say something along the lines of, "You know what, law is a lot like medicine. You probably wouldn't trust a podiatrist with a question about a heart condition. I would recommend hiring an attorney with expertise in that area.

---

[4]   The DOJ Honors program has some limitations on participation. *See Entry-Level Attorneys*, U.S. DEPT. OF J. (Jun. 1, 2022), https://www.justice.gov/legal-careers/honors-program-eligibility.

[5]   JUDICIAL CLERKSHIP FORUM: A CONVERSATION WITH 12 JUDGES, AMERICAN BAR ASSOCIATION JUDICIAL DIVISION LAWYERS CONFERENCE 29 (2015).

[6]   Yes, I am being sarcastic here.

But, if you have a question about appellate advocacy or constitutional law, I am all ears!"

I think many law students and most nonlawyers don't realize how diverse the legal profession is. And putting aside the ethical issues with answering the questions above, most attorneys who don't practice in a specific area would be hard pressed to give, on the fly (figuratively or literally), really useful legal advice outside of their practice areas. Plus, as my husband likes to say, free legal advice is normally worth what you pay for it.

This long-winded introduction to Reason #3 is both to get something off my chest that really bothers me and to tell you that as a clerk you will be exposed to all sorts of cases. If you don't know what you want to do with your legal career (see Reason #1), this exposure can help you identify the areas of law you find interesting. Maybe you thought you wanted to practice contract law, but during your federal appellate clerkship you find the immigration appeals that your judge handles to be particularly interesting. Or maybe you planned on being a prosecutor, but you clerk for the family law bench in state court and decide that is your passion. The opposite may also be true. Perhaps you wanted to practice family law, but during your clerkship year you handle too many nasty divorce appeals, which sours you to that area of law.

In short, a clerkship can change the trajectory of your legal career by exposing you to different types of legal practice. You might find that a class you thought was boring in law school turns out to be fun as a career. If this is your reason for clerking, then a general clerkship would be your best bet to maximize your exposure to a variety of legal questions.

Reason #4: It Exposes You to Many Different Attorneys

Throughout my more than 50 years as a member of the bar, one lesson has stood out as more important than all the others: A good personal reputation is the greatest asset a lawyer possesses.

~Judge Edward M. Ginsburg[7]

As a law clerk, you will get to see different types of attorneys and law firms. You will see attorneys in the courtroom, at oral argument or trial, and you will see their work product in court filings. Furthermore, you "see" their reputations before the court, since judges discuss amongst themselves and with their clerks the attorneys that frequently appear before them. A clerkship is a perfect opportunity to decide what type of lawyer you want to be in practice—both in terms of style and reputation.

Let me start first with style. There are multiple effective attorney styles. Justice Kagan once told the story of two lawyers who frequently appeared before the United States Supreme Court. One attorney could be described as "hot," when he would stand to argue: "the [Court] just throbs with energy. Everybody leans forward in their chairs. There is so much sort of tension and energy in the air, and then, you know, he's just tremendous and sort of knocking everything out of the ballpark and arguing with you."[8] The other was "calm, cool, and collected as can be, and just sort of cools down the temperature of the room and is Mr. Reasonable Man, and surely you have to believe everything he says because he says

---

[7]   Edward M. Ginsburg, *For an attorney, reputation is everything*, DETROIT LEGAL NEWS (Nov. 18, 2014), http://legalnews.com/detroit/1397150.

[8]   Nicole Etter, *Nine Lessons from Supreme Court Justice Elena Kagan*, GARGOYLE ALUMNI MAG. FOR THE UNIV. OF WIS. L. SCH. (Aug. 10, 2018), https://gargoyle. law.wisc.edu/2018/08/10/nine-lessons-from-supreme-court-justice-elena-kagan/.

it in such a calm kind of way, sort of slow, you know."[9] Despite their different styles, she called both attorneys "tremendous, tremendous advocates."[10] In a different interview she identified the "hot" lawyer as former Solicitor General Paul Clement and the "cool" lawyer as now-Judge Sri Srinivasan who sits on the Court of Appeals for the D.C. Circuit.[11]

When I teach oral argument, I tell my students that story and encourage them to "be your best you." If you are a "cool" attorney, you probably wouldn't be effective if you tried to be "hot," but you can observe other "cool" attorneys and learn how to be effective with that style.

Most clerkships offer plenty of opportunities to view attorney styles. Trial court clerkships provide many chances to watch attorneys argue motions and interact with juries, witnesses, and the judge. Furthermore, in talking about the trial with your judge, you will likely get a judicial perspective on the attorney's style. Appellate clerkships, if the court hears regular oral argument, will also offer a chance to see how attorneys argue with limited time on appeal and discuss with your judge what was effective in that argument.

Not only will you get to observe attorneys' speaking styles, but also their writing styles. At the appellate level, an attorney's written work product is far more important than oral argument— especially considering that not all cases are set for oral argument. As an appellate clerk, you will read a lot of briefs—both in cases set for argument and in cases that are decided without argument. You will quickly develop a keen eye for the styles of writing that

---

[9] *Id.*

[10] *Id.*

[11] Marcia Coyle, *Justice Kagan to Set Sight on New Target*, LEGAL TIMES (Mar. 17, 2014).

persuade, and those that don't. Likewise, you will probably hear firsthand from your judge what briefs and styles persuaded them.

While written work product isn't as important at trial court, especially at the state level, trial clerks still read their fair share of attorney work product. And, like your appellate counterparts, you will see what works, and what doesn't.

In addition to observing attorneys' argument and writing styles, you will also see how attorneys make and break their reputations. As the quote at the start of this section demonstrates, an attorney's reputation is everything. And a lost reputation is nearly impossible to regain. I once heard an attorney tell a story about a judge he knew who, at an oral argument, leaned over to the judge next to him and said, "you see that attorney, he lied to me 20 years ago."

As a clerk you will undoubtedly see ways that attorneys can damage their reputation. You will see attorneys who are untrustworthy and misrepresent the facts and the law. You will see attorneys who are late to court or file documents late. You will see attorneys who disregard court rules. You will see attorneys who exaggerate to make their points appear stronger.[12] And, you will see how judges and juries, and even other attorneys, respond to these types of attorneys.

On the flip side, you will also observe attorneys with stellar reputations. They are known in the legal community as ethical, reliable, trustworthy, and accurate. And you will see how judges, juries, and other attorneys respond favorably to them.

This information about attorneys will not only help you develop your own attorney style and reputation; it will also help you decide where to work. You probably don't want to work at a law firm known

---

[12]   If nothing else, viewing these sloppy attorneys should boost your confidence as a new attorney. Anyone can go to law school, but not all attorneys take their jobs seriously. If you do, you are already ahead of them.

for producing disreputable attorneys. Furthermore, if you are a trial court clerk, you may interact closely enough with attorneys to be able to ask them about their workplaces—about the culture, the work-life balance, and the pay and benefits. This information is extremely valuable as you try and decide where to work post-clerkship.

Reason #5: It Makes You a Better Lawyer

[E]x-law clerks . . . come out equipped far better than most to build a good *appellate argument . . . .*

~Karl Llewellyn[13]

Clerking helps you become a better lawyer. In fact, when I discuss the benefits of clerking with former clerks, most of the reasons that they give for why you should clerk generally fall under this heading. Let me explain.

First, clerking gives you insight into judicial decision-making. You will see what types of arguments, both written and oral, persuade your judge. You will observe how your judge approaches different arguments or issues that come before the court and how your judge makes decisions. When you get into practice, you will then understand what persuades both the judge you clerked for and judges in general. Depending on the level of clerkship and the interaction that you have with other judges on that same bench, you might also learn other judges' idiosyncrasies. This knowledge will help you craft persuasive (and hopefully) winning arguments in practice. You will avoid actions that you know annoy judges, and you will act with respect and deference to the court.

Second, clerking helps you understand the role of an attorney. I remember one time during my clerkship I was discussing a case with my judge. I was really sure that X was the key issue in the case,

---

[13] LLEWELLYN, *supra* note 1, at 322.

but the judge believed Y was more important. And, because he was the judge and the person who would participate in oral argument and vote at conference, it was his perspective that mattered (although he certainly considered my views too). See, as a law clerk you learn a very important lawyer lesson—you serve a principal, the judge, who ultimately decides a case or a matter before the court. In practice you will serve lots of principals, whether clients or senior partners (who are serving clients). Learning how to advise, but not, as one of my friends put it, "advance [your] own agenda or desired outcome" is a valuable lawyering lesson.

Third, you will learn how the court system works. Some of this knowledge might be specific to your jurisdiction—like the court rules. Some of it, however, can be very general. For example, as a trial court clerk you will learn how to build a record, and as an appellate clerk, you will learn how important that record is on appeal! You will also learn the various types of court filings and how to file them properly. And you will understand the key players in a courthouse (like the clerk and deputy clerk) and in a courtroom (like the court reporter). All of this information makes you more prepared to practice law, and the relationships you build with court and courtroom staff will be beneficial once you are in practice.

Fourth, you will gain confidence, which will make you a better lawyer. As I discussed in Reason #4, clerkships expose you to all sorts of attorney styles. You will see some pretty poor attorneys. And while you shouldn't get too haughty about your abilities (there are enough stuck-up lawyers in this world), you should be confident that, with work and practice, you can do this!

Reason #6: It Exposes You to Valuable Information That Will Make You Desirable to Employers

The judicial clerks really get to see, for lack of a better phrase, how the sausage is made. . . . You get to see every day the inner workings of the courts, what the judges are expecting by way of fillings and oral argument and presentation before the court. You have the great inside look at what to do and what not to do when you go out into practice.

~Judge Aimee R. Belgard[14]

All of the things listed in Reason #5 that make you a better lawyer, also make you more desirable to employers. When law firms hire graduates straight out of law school, they anticipate that these baby lawyers will need a fair amount of training and oversight. However, when they hire clerks, they get young lawyers who (1) know the local court rules and (2) know the idiosyncrasies of the judges in that jurisdiction. As one of my former students who clerked told me, "Trial and appellate practitioners become incredibly valuable to their firms when they can advise colleagues on how a judge may react to a motion/request and how the local rules work."

In addition to knowing the rules and the inner workings of the local court, employers also appreciate that the clerks they hire have had a good deal of writing experience. Nothing quite prepares you for practice like having a judge critique your writing! And, after a year or two of clerking you may find yourself adopting many of your judge's writing idiosyncrasies when you leave the clerkship.

---

[14] Njcourts, *Judicial Clerkship Program Webinar-June 3, 2020,* YOUTUBE, 33:38–34:06 (July 7, 2020), https://www.youtube.com/watch?v=pM5VQcBhh2s. At the time of this quote, Judge Belgard was Presiding Judge of the New Jersey Civil Division.

These valuable clerk attributes are why some law firms, as discussed in the previous chapter, may offer significant hiring bonuses to law clerks.

Reason #7: It Can Lead to a Lifelong Relationship with the Judge and Friendships with Clerks

Through the years I have leaned on Judge Aycock for career advice and sometimes personal advice. She's offered wise counsel but always left the ultimate decision to me. It was my life after all, and I would have to live with the decision. She celebrated my professional accomplishments. She sent hand-written notes and even flowers on big career events, such as my first trial and new jobs.

~Judge Kristi H. Johnson[15]

A frequently cited reason for clerking is the relationship you build with your judge and your co-clerks. Just think about it—you will be working closely with a seasoned attorney who reached such high levels in their career that they were appointed or elected to be a judge. Undoubtedly that person will have keen insights on how you should structure your legal career. In fact, this is one of the reasons I suggest clerking for someone who shares your interests, as I will discuss in Chapter 4.

Don't be shy about discussing your career aspirations with your judge. I think most judges view clerkships as an opportunity to mentor young lawyers—many served as clerks after law school and reaped the benefits of the mentoring experience. Judges are usually well-connected in their jurisdiction. They will have insight into the

---

[15] Kristi H. Johnson, *Chief Judge Sharion Aycock: Role Model, Mentor, and Friend*, 39 Miss. C. L. Rev. 381, 383 (2021).

key legal (and political) players and might even be willing to introduce you to attorneys or bring you along to bench and bar functions.

Not only will you build a relationship with your judge, but you will also get to know your co-clerks and, depending on the court set-up, other clerks for other judges. Just like your law school classmates, these co-clerks will become your professional colleagues as your career progresses. You might work together (or on opposite sides) on cases. You might work together at law firms or governmental agencies. They might even become judges. In short, cultivating a good relationship with your co-clerks will not only make your clerkship more enjoyable, it may reap career benefits down the road. You may even make lifelong personal friends who can also help you Bluebook tricky citations, give you insight on a different jurisdiction's rules, and celebrate career wins with you.

In addition to the co-clerks from your clerkship year, clerking can also help you build relationships with people who clerked for your judge in different years. To return to the secret menu analogy, clerking for a judge gives you insight into that judge's preferences and decision-making process. You know the judge's writing pet peeves and what the judge likes (and dislikes) at oral argument. You probably also know how the judge likes their coffee, what their favorite restaurant is, and their funny stories from the bench. Your judge's other clerks share that same information. They also share the judge's imprimatur of approval—"You clerked for Judge Ramirez, I did too. You must be ok."

Depending on how long your judge has been on the bench when you clerk, this broader network (or family) of previous clerks could be quite large. And, again, depending on the length of time, these previous clerks could be in senior positions that could benefit you as a junior attorney. They might be partners at firms where you are applying, or they might lead governmental agencies where you want to work. Even if they don't offer job connections, they can certainly offer career advice. As one of my former students told me, "My clerkship gave me a network of friends and colleagues spread out across the legal field in a variety firms/agencies/roles. It's great starting a career and already having such an expansive network."

My experience has been that most former clerks are happy to network with current or future clerks about their experiences. As an example, before I started my clerkship, I met a few attorneys who had clerked for my judge. They freely offered helpful advice, and one remains a professional connection to this day.

Reason #8: It Is Prestigious for Some Jobs

There are attorneys that you can meet, that become fond of you as a law clerk and decide, you know what, I'm gonna pass your name on to a particular firm that I think you would be perfect for or things of that nature.

~Judge Martha T. Mainor[16]

For some legal jobs, clerking is a major application boost. For example, most tenure-track law professors clerked after law school, often for a federal judge. Many appellate attorneys clerked, often for the court they later practice before. As I discussed in Chapter 2, some firms offer bonuses to associates who clerked, evidencing that clerkships are valued by law firms, especially Biglaw firms. Finally, many judges themselves served as clerks, again some for the court that they ultimately end up serving on. So, if your career aspirations involve academia, being a judge, or working in Biglaw in a litigation or appellate practice, clerking is a boost to your application.

---

[16]   Njcourts, *Judicial Clerkship Program Webinar-June 3, 2020*, YOUTUBE, 37:35-37:46 (July 7, 2020), https://www.youtube.com/watch?v=pM5VQcBhh2s.

Reason #9: You Can Improve the Court System

When I took the bench [in 2014], I was struck by how many law clerks are white and from privileged backgrounds. This is to the detriment of the legal profession (in which people from all walks of life should have a chance to rise to the top) and the judiciary (which benefits from having people with different perspectives involved in the decision-making process).

~Judge Vince Chhabria[17]

Yes, you read that heading correctly—by clerking you might be able to improve the court system. How?

First, if you are in a clerkship where you regularly interface with the public, like a trial court clerkship or an ALJ clerkships, you can improve the legal system by making people's experiences in court positive. People seek the help of courts to resolve difficult, weighty matters. When they arrive at the courthouse they may be angry, scared, frustrated, or worried. And while they want justice, they also want to be heard. You will assist the judge in making sure that parties, witnesses, and victims feel heard. Think of it like visiting the doctor—your experience is better if you are treated with dignity and respect. The same should be true of people who come to court. As a clerk, you can help that happen.

Second, you can improve the court system by helping your judge come to the right conclusion in a case. You might find that small detail or dispositive case that will help the court come to the right conclusion. And even if you don't find some unique detail or

---

[17] Cheyenne N. Chambers, *A Peek Behind the Curtain: The Inner-Workings of the Judiciary, and Why Judges Should Address the Lack of Diversity Amount Law Clerks*, APPELLATE ISSUES (2020), https://www.americanbar.org/groups/judicial/publications/appellate_issues/2020/winter/a-peek-behind-the-curtain/.

dispositive case, helping your judge through research and discussion is important and valuable work.

Third, if you are part of a group that is underrepresented in the legal profession, you can help improve the court system by diversifying it. While diversity has many facets, I want to focus on racial diversity. Blacks, Hispanics, Asians, Native Americans, and Hawaiian/Pacific Islanders are underrepresented in the legal profession as a whole and the judiciary in particular.[18] The state court numbers are staggering—at the state supreme court level, only "17 percent of justices are Black, Latino, Asian American, or Native American. By contrast, people of color make up almost 40 percent of the U.S. population."[19] Considering that I was one of three Native Americans in my 1L class, I am not surprised by these statistics. Improved law school admissions numbers for students of color will help persons of color be better represented in the legal profession, but more racially-diverse judicial clerks will help improve the judiciary as a whole. As I noted above, many judges started their legal careers as clerks. Furthermore, as a clerk you can speak to other students of colors about pursuing judicial clerkships.

BUT, Not Everything is Rainbows and Butterflies or Champagne and Caviar

Do your homework . . . . Google the judge. Are they well-regarded? Are they often reversed? . . . . If the judge is

---

[18]   Laura Bagby, *ABA Profile of the Legal Profession: Diversity and Well-Being*, 2CIVILITY (Aug. 13, 2020), https://www.2civility.org/aba-profile-of-the-legal-profession-diversity-and-well-being/.

[19]   Janna Adelstein & Alicia Bannon, *State Supreme Court Diversity—April 2021 Update*, BRENNAN CENTER FOR JUSTICE (May 25, 2022), https://www.brennancenter.org/our-work/research-reports/state-supreme-court-diversity-april-2021-update.

local, go observe him or her in court so you can get a sense of their temperament.

~Judge Jerald Bagley[20]

Despite how great I think clerkships are, I do occasionally hear arguments against clerkships. In the interest of full disclosure, I am going to discuss and refute the three key arguments I hear most often against clerking.

Reason #1: I Just Want to Start Working

After three years of law school, more than a decade of watching every lawyer show worth watching,[21] and countless hours listening to every true crime podcast, you are ready to get to work. I get it. But, at the risk of demeaning my own profession, law school doesn't teach you everything. One of the key lessons I learned in my clerkship was how little I actually knew about the practice of law. Law school taught me how to think differently and how to approach problems, but I knew very little about the practical aspects of practicing law. It was humbling (and important) for me to learn in my clerkship year how much I still had to learn about being a lawyer. I was fortunate to have great mentors in my judge and co-clerks (all of whom had clerked for at least a year before I joined our chambers).

Thankfully, in the last decade or so law schools have made a concerted effort to teach more practical skills. But despite this positive change, students still graduate law school with much to learn about practicing law. For the reasons I outline above, I think a year of working under a judge can teach you much about being a

---

[20]   Deborah Schneider, *Judicial Clerkships for Everyone*, 35 STUDENT LAW. 18, 23 (2006).

[21]   This list is highly debatable, and I dare not enter the fray. I have, however, blogged on good appellate lawyer movies. Tessa L. Dysart, *Best Appellate Movies*, APPELLATE ADVOCACY BLOG (Jan. 9, 2017), https://lawprofessors.typepad.com/appellate_advocacy/2017/01/best-appellate-movies.html.

good lawyer. So, even if you want to get working, you will work better and smarter after clerking a year.

Reason #2: I Just Want to Make Money, and Clerkships Don't Pay That Much

You look at the opportunity that is created by the position . . . . It's been my experience that when you look at your professional life, you have to look at your entire professional activities, not just the money. . . . I've always taken the position that if you like what you do, the money will follow. A lot of the dividends of being a law clerk pay off years later when you transition to another job.

~Judge Stephen McNamee[22]

After three years of law school and more than a decade of watching shows where lawyers live lavishly, you are ready to start making money and some clerkships don't pay well. Clerkship pay is a problem, and one that I hope states fix, since they are the main offenders. It certainly behooves states to provide their judges with top-notch clerks. Clerks help the judges do their work—i.e., that little task of interpreting the law—and clerkships provide excellent training for the young lawyers who will ultimately work in the state. But, despite the sometimes-low salaries for clerks, I still think clerking is worth it. The connections, experience, mentorship, and learning opportunities make up for the low salary. And you may receive a bonus at a law firm after you finish your clerkship. Other firms offer a higher starting salary for former clerks. Finally, clerking may open employment opportunities that would not have been open to you but for the clerkship.

---

22   Tom R. Arterburn, *The Clerkship Club*, 30 STUDENT LAW. 18, 21 (2001) (second omission in the original).

If you are really concerned about making money when you graduate from law school, let me offer one other piece of advice. This may sound harsh, but it comes from my own personal experience and that of seeing countless law students over the years. Here it is: Live like a student and not a lawyer when you are in law school. Law school is expensive. The fewer debts you incur as a law student, the more flexibility you will have to pick the career you want, not the career that pays the most money. That means that you might need to forgo the newest technology, the nicer car, the fancy restaurants, and the designer clothes while you are a student. But frugality as a student can help you live like the lawyers you saw on TV after you graduate or have the public interest career you want, rather than feeling pushed into a firm job you may not want. Being stuck in a high-paying job (the "golden handcuffs") makes you feel powerless, not powerful like the attorney you went to law school to be.

Reason #3: I Don't Want to Work for a Tyrant

After three years of law school and more than a decade of watching tough judges on TV, you are really sure that you don't want to clerk for one of those judges. Few people want to work for a tyrant. I say "few," because I know people who clerked for judges with "tough" reputations in part because those judges were considered "feeder" judges, meaning their former clerks were often hired as United States Supreme Court clerks. That, however, was not the clerkship experience that I wanted, and I suspect it isn't the experience that most readers of this book want.

Fortunately, in real life, most judges aren't tyrants. They may be particular about research and writing, but they know that you, as a new attorney, are still learning.

So how do you avoid working for a tyrant? The key is to do your research on judges, which I will discuss in the next two chapters.

With a little due diligence on your part, you can often avoid applying to judges who are known tyrants to their clerks.

Short & Happy!

- Clerkships will make you a better attorney.
- Clerkships provide a "family" of mentors and professional (and personal) friends—your judge and the other clerks.
- The benefits of clerking outweigh the downsides.

CHAPTER 4

WHERE Should You Clerk?

Now that I have explained what kinds of clerkships are available and convinced you why you should clerk, it is time to look at where you should clerk.

This "where" step is an important one in the process. Strong clerkship applications take time to put together. And as I will discuss in Chapter 5, each clerkship application should be tailored to that specific judge. Sending identical applications (minus the salutation in the cover letter) to every judge in a jurisdiction is an ineffective strategy, as it won't make your application stand out among the hundreds that judges' receive. Taking time to carefully consider where you should clerk will help you create strong, individualized applications that are more likely to reap positive results.

To help you decide where to clerk, I will pose four questions that you need to ask yourself about clerking before finalizing your application list. I will discuss these questions in the order you should ask them, although in many ways they are interrelated.

Also, as you consider these questions, be honest about your answers. If you are uncertain about how to answer the questions, reach out to a trusted professor or your career services counselor.

Question #1—How Strong Is Your Application?

I don't have any criteria [for clerks] that say you have to be top 5 or 10 percent. . . . People can have other skills that don't test well yet still make them tremendous lawyers. I know that if you're the top at your law school, that's not necessarily going to make you the best lawyer in town.

~Justice Ann Scott Timmer[1]

The first question you need to ask yourself is how strong your application is relative to other applicants. This assessment will help you determine what level of court you should apply to.

This is perhaps the hardest step, since, as I discuss below, there are factors beyond grades that make an application competitive. Plus, given the secret menu that surrounds law school, you as a law student might not know if your grades make your application competitive. This is especially true if you start thinking about clerking during your 1L year, when you have limited grades and you might not have a class rank.

If you evaluate the strength of your application on your own, chances are your evaluation will fall into one of two categories. You might take the "grandma approach," meaning you overestimate the strength of your application, just like your proud grandma might. Or you might take the "imposter approach," meaning you underestimate the strength of your application. Either way, this is

---

[1]   Tom R. Arterburn, *The Clerkship Club*, 30 STUDENT LAW. 18, 20 (2001) (alteration in the original).

the step where you will most benefit from reading this book and talking to a trusted professor, mentor, or career services counselor.

Let me give you a few generalizations to help you evaluate the strength of your application. These are definitely generalizations, but hopefully they give you a place to start:

- If you are a student at a top five law school and you have good "grades," which I would define as passes and high passes with very few low passes, you should be competitive for all federal and state clerkships with the exception of known "feeder" federal judges, who probably want to see a lot of high passes.[2]

- If you are a *top* student (top 5-10% in your class) at a top 50 law school, you might be competitive for a federal appellate clerkship. The higher ranked your law school, the higher ranked you are in the class, and the more connections you have (see Question 4), the more competitive your application will be at the federal appellate level.

- If you are a ranked first or second in your class at any other law school, you might be competitive for a federal appellate clerkship. The connections discussed in this chapter will be imperative.

- If you are a *top* student (top 5-10% in your class) at any law school, you will be competitive at the federal district court level, especially local federal district courts. Students that fall into the 10-20% may be competitive too, especially if their law

---

[2] Most of the top law schools have eschewed letter grades in favor of a pass system. Evan Jones, *Which Law Schools are Pass/Fail?*, LAWSCHOOLI (Dec. 21, 2020, 10:19 AM), https://lawschooli.com/law-schools-passfail/.

school is higher ranked or they have significant connections.

- If you are in the top 25% of your class, you will be competitive at state supreme courts, especially if you have connections to the state or the judge.

- If you are in the top 30% of your class, you will be competitive at the state supreme court in the state that your law school is located in.

- If you are top 40% of your class, you will be competitive for the state intermediate appellate court, especially in the state that your law school is located in or in a state that you are connected to. Students below the top 40% may also be competitive if they have significant connections.

- For state trial courts the qualifications will vary by jurisdiction, but it helps to be in the same state and have connections to the court. Strong application materials, such as strong letters of recommendation, can make up for less than stellar academics.

- For administrative or specialty court clerkships, students in the top 25% from top 50 law schools are generally more competitive. But having previous work experience in the subject matter of the court's jurisdiction can boost an application from a lower ranked student. Students in the top 10% from lower-ranked schools can also be competitive.

- For international and Tribal court clerkships it also helps to have a connection to the country, court, or Tribe.

This list is by no means comprehensive, and the strength of your application will depend on other factors, especially those discussed under Question 4. And, if you are applying for clerkships after a year or two of work, your class and law school rank will matter less. But I hope this list gives you a starting point to evaluate your application.

You might read this list and think, "You said that there was a clerkship for everyone. I am in the bottom of my class at a lower ranked law school. What clerkships are out there for me?" Good question. Generally, the least competitive clerkships are the state trial court clerkships, especially in the states that pay poorly. You will need to focus on building a strong application, with strong letters of recommendation. I will discuss these materials in Chapter 5. You should also try to improve your grades and find judges with connections to you or your school. Finally, regardless of this list, don't take yourself out of the clerkship running. You might be surprised how your application materials will catch a judge's attention. I just give you this list to help you think about where you are most likely to have success and where to best target your applications.

Question #2—Does the "Why" You Want to Clerk Point You in the Direction of a Particular Court or Judge?

Sometimes why you want to clerk will point you in the direction of applying to a particular court or judge. If you want to have a state appellate practice, then applying to the state intermediate appellate or supreme court would be beneficial to your career. If you want a federal practice, then you should focus on federal trial and appellate courts. If you are interested in working in an area of law that involves significant agency interaction, you should see if that agency has ALJs who hire clerks. If you are interested in international or Tribal law, focus on clerkships with those courts.

Other "whys" might also factor into the equation. If you are clerking to transition to a particular type of practice or location, your choices will be limited by those factors, although a general state or federal clerkship could help you transition to several different types of practice.

Question #3—Are There Any Geographic Limitations on Where You Can Clerk?

As much as you might want to clerk in the remote regions of Alaska or near the beaches of Hawaii, it might not be practical or possible. You might have obligations that require you to stay in a specific location or state. If so, focus your judge search on those locations. Even with those limitations, you should still have a wide range of clerkship opportunities, depending on the location. These opportunities can even include ALJ clerkships, particularly Immigration ALJ clerkships, depending on the location.

If you want to clerk but you attended a lower-ranked law school, you might be geographically limited to your law school's location, since this is where your law school is better known and likely has alumni on the bench. This doesn't mean you can't apply outside these limitations, but it does mean that your application might be more competitive in an area where your law school is better known.

Question #4—Do You Have Any Connections to Judges?

My office was small . . . . As such, I was more concerned than anything else about having clerks with whom I would enjoy working at close quarters. To the student . . . this meant being himself or herself both on paper and during the interview so that I would get as accurate an

*impression as possible of what the person would be like
to work with.*

~Judge Frank Sullivan, Jr.[3]

This is my favorite question to ask. In my opinion, this is the question that many people underestimate, misunderstand, or ignore. Before I launch into the specifics of this question, let's remember the working environment for most judges. Most judges lead a relatively solitary professional life. Appellate judges do the bulk of their work in their chambers, with their small staff of clerks and a judicial assistant as company. Even if their chambers are in a court building with other judges, on many courts, judge only discuss cases before oral argument with their own chambers staff, not the other judges. Although trial judges have more interaction with the public, bar, and court staff, they still rely only on their clerks for confidential discussions about the matters before them.

It is important to remember the working environment for judges because it reiterates how important "fit" is for clerkship applications. You might be the best law student at the best law school in the country, but if you won't fit well into the chambers environment, most judges won't hire you. This is why, as we will discuss in Chapter 5, the interview is so important. It is also why connections are important. By connections I don't mean just how many judges you know personally, although it certainly helps to know judges. I mean interests or experiences that you and a judge have in common. Below are a few questions you should ask to find possible connections with judges. I will then explain where you can find the answers to these questions.

---

[3]   Darhiana Mateo Tellez, *Clerkship Confidential*, 43 STUDENT LAW. 28, 30 (2015).

Do You Share an Alma Mater (Undergrad or Law or Other)?

> *The vast majority of my clerks so far have been [from my law school alma mater] . . . . I have come to trust [it] to prepare my clerks to be skilled writers and researchers, and to think critically and creatively about the legal issues that come before my court.*

~Judge C.J. Williams[4]

Many people have fond memories of their alma maters. They root for the football team, attend reunions and homecoming, and yell "Go Wildcats" when they see a Arizona license plate outside the state.[5] Judges are no different, except maybe for Justice Thomas who notoriously dislikes his alma mater, Yale Law School.[6] This means that when you are compiling the list of judges to whom you want to apply, you should look at judges who graduated from one of your schools, whether college, grad school, law school, or even a particularly tight-knit high school.

I advocate for defining alma mater loosely. When I chaired the Clerkship Committee at the University of Arizona James E. Rogers College of Law, my research assistant put together a list of every judge who attended any of the colleges at the University of Arizona, including undergraduate and masters programs. My reasoning was that a judge who received their undergraduate degree from the University of Arizona, but their law degree from a school in California, could still hold some loyalty or connection to Arizona law

---

4   Suzi Morales, *Iowa Law alums share their paths to the judiciary*, UNIVERSITY OF IOWA COLLEGE OF LAW (Sep. 23, 2021), https://law.uiowa.edu/news/2021/09/iowa-law-alums-share-their-paths-judiciary.

5   This happened to my husband recently when he was filling up our car at a Costco in Reno, Nevada. Although I teach at the University of Arizona, neither of us claim it as our alma mater.

6   Nathan Harden, *Why Clarence Thomas Hates Yale*, THE COLLEGE FIX (Jan. 15, 2013, 10:27 AM), https://www.thecollegefix.com/clarence-thomas-breaks-7-year-silence-to-mock-yale/.

grads who applied for clerkships. Likewise, as an undergraduate alumna of Willamette University, I would have no qualms about mentioning that connection if I were applying to clerk for a judge who attended Willamette Law School, but not Willamette undergrad. If you head up a law school career services office, you should have a list of every judge (state, federal, Tribal) who graduated from your school (however broadly you define "school"). I will offer a trick for finding those federal judges in this chapter, and the research librarians at your law library can probably help find the state judges if your alumni office does not have the information.

Does the Judge Have Other Connections with Your School, Such as Teaching a Class at the School or Participating in School Activities?

It is my personal system to disqualify my interns from serving as my law clerks. Most of the judges are just the opposite and look at internships as a preview of the person to come. . . . If you get to intern in any of the judges' chambers, state or federal, it is good experience.

~Judge Charles Day[7]

Even if they aren't graduates of a particular law school, some judges still participate in activities at various law schools, especially ones located nearby their chambers. They might teach a class or seminar, guest lecture, speak at lunch events, hire interns, or judge intramural competitions. These are all opportunities to build a connection with the judge, and, when possible, you should take advantage of them. And, it goes without saying, that you should put your best foot forward in the class, at the lecture, or in the competition.

---

[7]   JUDICIAL CLERKSHIP FORUM: A CONVERSATION WITH 12 JUDGES, AMERICAN BAR ASSOCIATION JUDICIAL DIVISION LAWYERS CONFERENCE 19 (2015).

One special note about internships. Interning for a judge is often a great clerkship try-out. Some judges don't require their interns to have the same academic credentials as their clerks, so if your application is borderline, excelling at an internship could help your clerkship application be more competitive. However, owing to their mission to train as many junior lawyers as possible, a few judges have a policy of not hiring former interns as clerks to give more students chambers experiences. Thus, before you accept an internship with a judge, be sure to check the judge's policy about hiring interns as clerks.

Has the Judge Hired Clerks from Your School?

If your law school isn't highly ranked, one way to find a connection with a judge is to look for judges who have previously hired clerks from your school. This is especially true with judges who are not local to your school and may not be generally informed about your alma mater. Hopefully, the previous clerk from your school left a good impression with the judge, so the judge will look favorably on your application.

If this is a connection you want to pursue, I would encourage you to work with your career services office and alumni office to identify these judges and former clerks. If the former clerk is open to it, contact them to discuss their clerkship experience. Just keep in mind that the conversation will probably be reported back to chambers. This could be to your benefit if the conversation goes well!

Do You Belong to or Participate in Similar Legal Organizations as the Judge?

I'm looking for a subjective fit with my chambers. I don't have a litmus test. I don't require participation in the Federalist Society, for example, but I'm looking for a general, philosophical fit with my chambers and my own decision-making approach because I don't want to be fighting with my law clerks all term.

~Judge Diana Sykes[8]

One great way to connect with judges is through legal organizations. As you will discover in law school, there are a host of legal organizations to join. These organizations cover a range of topics—from constitutional interpretation to personal identity. Some of the prominent organizations include the American Inns of Court, the Federalist Society, the American Constitution Society, the American Civil Liberties Union, the American Bar Association, the Christian Legal Society, the Animal Legal Defense Fund, and the National Lawyers Guild.

These organizations are typically made up of lawyers, although many of the organizations offer student memberships and have student chapters at law schools. These organizations may also boast judges as current or former members. The ethical rules in some jurisdictions prevent judges from being members of these organizations after they assume the bench. Regardless of their membership status, judges still participate in events for these organizations, including national conferences.

Attending national conferences for these organizations as a student is a great way to network with judges and local lawyers. Some of these organizations let students attend for free as volunteers who help with registration and other organizational tasks. I attended the Federalist Society National Lawyers Conference as a student volunteer when I was in law school, and I met several interesting and prominent lawyers and judges, including a U.S. Supreme Court Justice.

---

[8]   David R. Stras, Diane S. Sykes, & James A. Wynn Jr., *Panel Discussion: Judges' Perspectives on Law Clerk Hiring, Utilization, and Influence*, 98 MARQ. L. REV. 441, 445-46 (2014).

Being a member or leader in the student chapters of these organizations is also a way to build a connection with a judge who, prior to assuming the bench, was actively involved in the same organization. In some instances, it also signals to the judge that you share, for example, a similar approach to constitutional interpretation. Some judges prefer to hire clerks who share their legal philosophy, so demonstrating this connection in your application materials can be important for those judges.

Do You Share Non-Legal Interests with the Judge?

I recently hired a clerk who served in the Peace Corps. It wasn't legal experience, but it showed a strong work ethic and sense of commitment.

~Judge Jose Fuentes[9]

You can also build connections with judges by showing that you share non-legal interests. Perhaps you were both Eagle Scouts. Perhaps you both played college water polo. Perhaps you both participated in theater productions in college. Perhaps you both love running marathons. Perhaps you both volunteer at the Humane Society. Perhaps you both have your ham radio licenses. Before you dismiss this as silly, remember again how closely a judge works with their clerks.

Our extra-curricular activities say a lot about what we value, and in many of the examples I gave above, it also says a lot about our work ethic, grit, and determination. A judge who shares your values in one area might think, "Gosh, we have a lot in common, I bet this person would be a good fit for my chambers." They might also say, "Wow, I know how hard it is to be an Eagle Scout or run

---

[9]   Deborah Schneider, *Judicial Clerkships for Everyone*, 35 STUDENT LAW. 18, 23 (2006).

marathons. That the applicant reached this level of success says a lot about their character and determination."

This type of connection may not help your application if you don't meet the judge's minimum qualifications, but it could boost your application and get you an interview if you're up against similarly situated applicants who don't share that interest.

Do You Share Personal Characteristics?

You can draw connections with judges based on other shared personal connections. Perhaps you are both first generation law students or college graduates. Perhaps you both grew up in a rural area. Perhaps you both did a missionary trip to South America. These connections can make your application stand out amongst the vast pool of applicants.

Do You Have Similar Career Aspirations as the Judge?

Another connection that you can draw with a judge is shared career aspirations. Perhaps the judge was a prominent water law attorney, and you want to practice in that field. Or maybe the judge was a dedicated public defender, and you want to go into criminal defense work. Or maybe the judge was a politician before being seated on the bench, and you want to go into politics. As I discussed in Chapter 3, one of the reasons to clerk is for the mentorship relationship you can build with the judge. What better mentor then one who did what you want to do! Think of the career advice they can share with you and the connections they will have with attorneys who still practice in the field.

This type of connection is especially important to highlight in a cover letter, since it explains why you want to clerk for that specific judge, rather than for other judges on the same court. It is also an easy connection to find, since most judges list past employment in their court biographies. Still, mentioning this connection in a cover letter shows the judge you did your due diligence in researching them and distinguishing them from other judges.

Finding the Connections

How do you find these connections without appearing to be a cyber-stalker? There are several sources that can help you research judges, and these sources often include (if the judge cares to share it) both personal and career information about the judge. The value of these sources depends, in part, on why you want to clerk. For example, if you are looking for a judge who shares your love of originalism, you probably want to focus on judges appointed by Republican presidents and governors. (Although be careful—the politics of the appointing president/governor and the judge do not always track!) Alternatively, if you just want a clerkship in your home state of Oregon, your focus will be on sources that list judges by geographical location.

Here are some of my favorite resources for finding judges and connections with judges.

Federal Judicial Center Advanced Judge Search[10]

The Federal Judicial Center (FJC) is the research and educational arm of the federal court system.[11] It maintains a searchable database of all Article III federal judges since 1789. If you click on the advanced search option you can search by various characteristics, including:

---

[10]   *Biographical Directory of Article III Federal Judges, 1789-present*, FEDERAL JUDICIAL CENTER, https://www.fjc.gov/history/judges/search/advanced-search (last visited Aug. 26, 2022).

[11]   *About the FJC*, FEDERAL JUDICIAL CENTER, https://www.fjc.gov/about (last visited Aug. 26, 2022).

- Court;

- Nominating president;

- Gender;

- Race or ethnicity;

- Education (both undergraduate and graduate); and

- Professional experience.

You can also limit your search to sitting judges, since you know that Chief Justice John Marshall isn't currently hiring clerks.

For example, I searched for all sitting judges who graduated from the University of Arizona James E. Rogers College of Law. Here were my results (next page):

Advanced Search Criteria

Enter Search Criteria

▾ Court

☐ Supreme Court of the United States
  ▸ U.S. Courts of Appeals

  ▸ U.S. District Courts

  ▸ U.S. Circuit Courts

  ▸ Other Federal Courts

☐ Limit to Chief and Presiding Justices and Judges

▸ Nomination / Confirmation / Commission

▸ Senior Status / Termination

▾ Personal Characteristics and Background

Gender

[- both - ▾]

▸ Race or Ethnicity

▸ Other Federal Judicial Service

Education

[University of Arizona College of Law-t]

Professional Experience

[Contains exact phrase ▾]

[   ]

▸ Research Resources

▾ Limit to Sitting Judges

○ All Judges
◉ All Sitting Judges
○ Active Judges
○ Senior Status Judges

Search Results

Number of judges matching the search criteria: 11

Baldock, Bobby Ray
Bury, David C.
Collins, Raner Christercunean
Hinderaker, John Charles
Jorgenson, Cindy K.
Márquez, Rosemary
McNamee, Stephen M.
Rash, Scott Hugh
Reiss, Christina Clair
Teilborg, James A.
Zapata, Frank R.

Clicking on a judge's name brings up a brief biographical sketch:

Collins, Raner Christercunean

Born 1952 in Malvern, AR

Federal Judicial Service:
Judge, U.S. District Court for the District of Arizona
Nominated by William J. Clinton on May 11, 1998, to a seat vacated by William D. Browning. Confirmed by the Senate on July 31, 1998, and received commission on August 3, 1998. Served as chief judge, 2013-2018. Assumed senior status on March 4, 2019.

Education:
Arkansas Polytechnic College (now Arkansas Tech University), B.A., 1973
University of Arizona College of Law (now James E. Rogers College of Law), J.D., 1975

Professional Career:
Pima County [Arizona] Attorney's Office, 1975-1981; law clerk, 1975-1976; trial attorney, 1976-1981
Magistrate, Tucson [Arizona] City Court, 1981-1983
County attorney, Pima County, Arizona, 1983-1985
Judge pro tem, Superior Court of Arizona, Pima County, 1985-1988
Judge, Superior Court of Arizona, Pima County, 1988-1998

I am a pretty big research nerd and could spend hours thinking up all sorts of fun searches to run, but as law students you probably don't have time for that! I recommend using this search engine to initially cull your list of judges, especially if you care about things like nominating president, court, education, or practice experience.

Almanac of the Federal Judiciary

The *Almanac of the Federal Judiciary* is, perhaps, the best resource for researching federal judges and finding the connections that I discussed above. I relied heavily on the paper version of the *Almanac* when I was applying to clerkships. There is now a handy online version that is even better than the paper version. (Seriously, I am a bit jealous!) What makes the *Almanac* so great is that it is a one stop shop for key information about federal judges. And, the newer the judge, the more information available.

Like the FJC search engine, the *Almanac* allows you to search by court, so you can, for example, identify all the judges, including magistrate judges, in a certain judicial district. When you click on a particular judge's name, you pull up a wealth of information about that judge. Of all the databases I know, the *Almanac* has the most comprehensive biographical data on judges, including volunteer activities, honors, awards, and publications. It also includes information on the judge's noteworthy rulings. My favorite feature in the Almanac is that it provides lawyers' evaluations and comments about the judge. These evaluations can help you gauge the personality of the judge and, hopefully, avoid judges who have reputations for being tyrants.

For newer judges, the *Almanac* includes a link to download the judge's Senate Judiciary Committee Biographical Questionnaire. When available, the *Almanac* also allows you to download a judge's financial disclosure reports. I will discuss confirmation documents below, but, in short, Senate Questionnaires give you a tremendous amount of information about a judge's professional life, and even some about their personal life. It is a great way to find connections including membership in shared organizations, both legal and non-legal, and geographic connections.

The *Almanac*, however, is not a free source. But your law school should have access to it as either a print or electronic resource. Sometimes finding the database that includes the *Almanac* can be tricky. If you are unsure if your law school library has access to the *Almanac*, ask the library staff.

Court Websites

The two sources described above are great tools for researching federal judges. Unfortunately, for the state bench there isn't one great comprehensive source. So, as a starting place for those courts, I would recommend using court websites.

Most court websites will provide a list of the judges on that court and brief biographies for the judges. Consider this example from one of Arizona's intermediate courts. Under the menu item "Court Information" is a list of the judges. Clicking on a judge's name takes me to that judge's biography, which includes, among other things, when the judge was appointed or elected, in some cases who appointed the judge, the judge's educational background, the judge's prior work experience, and, in some instances, personal information about the judge.

Kent E. Cattani

Judge Kent Cattani was appointed to the Arizona Court of Appeals on February 9, 2013. After serving for 2 years as Vice Chief Judge, he was elected Chief Judge in June 2021.

At the time of Judge Cattani's appointment to the court, he was serving as Arizona's Solicitor General, overseeing criminal appeals, capital litigation, and civil appeals at the Arizona Attorney General's Office.

Judge Cattani earned his J.D. from the University of California at Berkeley in 1985, and he worked as an associate at Jennings, Strouss & Salmon, and Beus, Gilbert & Morrill in Phoenix prior to joining the Attorney General's Office in 1991. For the next 22 years, he represented the State of Arizona in state and federal court, handling death penalty post-conviction proceedings in trial courts throughout the State, briefing over 200 appellate cases, and arguing more than 95 cases in the Arizona Supreme Court, the Ninth Circuit, and the United States Supreme Court. He also assumed supervisory responsibilities as a Unit Chief, Section Chief, Division Chief, and Solicitor General.

As an Assistant Attorney General, Judge Cattani provided testimony to the United States Senate and House of Representatives Judiciary Committees regarding federal habeas and death penalty issues, and he helped draft legislation and worked with the Arizona legislature in addressing a variety of criminal law issues. He has also lectured extensively both locally and nationally on criminal law and federal habeas issues, and he is a co-editor of the Arizona Appellate Handbook.

Judge Cattani led the Attorney General's efforts to collaborate with the defense bar in studying lessons learned from DNA exonerations. Additionally, he chaired the Attorney General's DNA Task Force from 2006 – 2009, and he is the Vice Chair of Arizona's Forensic Science Advisory Committee formed as a result of recommendations by the Task Force. He also serves at the federal level as Vice Chair of the Legal Resources Committee of the Organization of Scientific Area Committees, which is tasked with promulgating standards for forensic science disciplines in the United States.

You might think this website information is too basic, but you can use it to ascertain the political party of the judge's appointing governor, whether the judge graduated from your alma mater, the judge's previous practice area, legal and nonlegal organizations that the judge belongs to, and even (in some instances) where the judge attends religious services![12]

Westlaw's Litigation Analytics

Westlaw's Litigation Analytics also offers information on both state and federal judges.

I am a bit loathe to explain Litigation Analytics in great detail, since I find that Westlaw and Lexis frequently change the appearances (and even the names) of their databases. But I will give you a general overview of the resource as it exists at the time of the writing of this book.

In general, this resource is useful for finding biographical information on specific judges, as well as getting an insight into their judicial philosophy. This source allows you to search by judge's name, and it provides a biographical sketch of the judge, including articles the judge has written and previous employment experiences. You could also search for cases the judge undertook as a lawyer.

In addition to a biographical sketch, the source provides an overview of the judge's decisions, including how those decisions fared on appeal. You can also view which other opinions the judge cites in their own opinions. And there is a tab for references to that judge, which can include news references. For example, according to Litigation Analytics, Justice Elena Kagan most often cites opinions written by the late-Justice Antonin Scalia. Her most frequently cited case is *United States v. Detroit Timber & Lumber Company*,[13] which

---

[12]   For that last point check out the biographies of justices on the Georgia Supreme Court. *See, e.g., Justice Carla Wong McMillian*, SUPREME COURT OF GEORGIA, https://www.gasupreme.us/court-information/biographies/justice-carla-wong-mcmillian/ (last visited Aug. 26, 2022).

[13]   200 U.S. 321 (1906).

is a semi-false result since it is cited after the syllabus in Supreme Court opinions to explain that the syllabus is not part of the Court's opinion.[14]

Because this resource requires you to search by judge, I would use this resource to either cull an existing list of judges or find more information about a judge prior to an interview.

Lexis Litigation Profile Suite & Lexis Litigation Analytics

Lexis Litigation Profile Suite works much like Westlaw's Litigation Analytics. You can use it to search for a specific judge, and it includes both trial and appellate judges. It does not appear to allow you to search by court.

Generally, the information in the Lexis database is similar to what you will find in Westlaw's database. Lexis has less information on case trends, but more secondary and news materials. The Lexis database also has less biographical information on a judge, but it does include a more easily accessible list of the judge's cases.

Lexis also has a resource conveniently (confusingly) called Litigation Analytics. It appears to only cover federal district court judges, but it contains detailed information in line with Westlaw's Litigation Analytics.

Confirmation or Appointment Documents

Federal judges are nominated by the President to their position, but before they can be formally appointed, they must be confirmed by the Senate. Under modern practice, the Senate Judiciary Committee asks that nominees fill out extensive questionnaires. It then holds confirmation hearings for the nominees, where the Senators on the Committee ask the nominee

---

[14]   *Becerra v. Empire Health Found.*, 142 S. Ct. 2354, 2355 (2022).

questions. Before I became a law professor, I worked on judicial confirmations for both the Senate Judiciary Committee and the Department of Justice's Office of Legal Policy (OLP). Attorneys at OLP shepherd nominees through the confirmation process.

Senate Questionnaires tell you a lot about a judge, including the judge's professional work history, volunteer activity, speeches, articles written, and key cases as an attorney. Hearing transcripts, depending on the questions from the Committee, can often tell you about the judge's judicial philosophy.

For recent nominees, you can find Senate Questionnaires on the Senate Judiciary Committee website.[15] For other nominees, the Senate Questionnaire, along with the hearing transcript, is available as a published Senate Hearing Report. Finding these documents can be a bit tricky, so I recommend working with a law librarian. I use the Proquest Congressional database to find Senate Hearing Reports.

For state judges who are appointed, you may be able to find similar documents. For example, in Arizona the state nominating commission makes current questionnaires available online.[16] Much like the federal questionnaire, this questionnaire provides important information about the candidates. It behooves career services offices in states that release questionnaires to download them and keep them on file for future student applicants.

---

[15] Currently, Questionnaires dating back to 2009 are available on the Senate Judiciary Committee website. *Library*, COMMITTEE ON THE JUDICIARY, https://www. judiciary.senate.gov/library?PageNum_rs=29&c=all&type=committee_questionnaire (last visited Aug. 26, 2022) (showing Senate Questionnaires dating back to June 23, 2009).

[16] *Vacancy Applications*, ARIZONA JUDICIAL BRANCH, https://www.azcourts.gov/ jnc/Vacancy-Applications (last visited Aug. 26, 2022).

Law School Resources

> *David Siegel, that professor I worked for, called me and remembered I had been interested in a clerkship, and said, "Send your resume to Judge Kaye. She's looking for a clerk." So I thought, why not? . . . And she hired me . . . . And much, much later she told me, "I really never wanted to hire you, but David Siegel just wouldn't stop calling me," which is a nice lesson about how you can really help someone's career.*

~Judge Michael J. Garcia[17]

Your law school may also have resources to help you find information about judges. Here are a few places to look:

Career Services Offices. The career services office at your law school should have resources to help you through the clerkship process. Ideally, the office will have a list of judges who graduated from your law school and a list of alumni who have clerked and who are willing to talk to future applicants. The office may also have various guides full of helpful information. Some offices also have a specific career counselor who focuses on clerkships. If, as a 1L, you know that you want to clerk, I would recommend connecting with the clerkship advisor or another career advisor as soon as possible.

Even if the career services office at your law school does not have a wealth of clerkship information, you can find publicly available information from other law school career services offices. I have sourced some of this material in the footnotes of this book. A few well-worded internet searches will yield a number of free guides.

---

[17] *Judgment Calls with Hon. David F. Levi*, BOLCH JUDICIAL INSTITUTE DUKE LAW (Mar. 10, 2022), https://judicialstudies.duke.edu/2022/03/judgment-calls-michael-j-garcia/.

Student Organizations. Some student organizations, especially ones with a national presence, maintain clerkships guides or support their members who are seeking clerkships. This is especially true with student organizations that focus on judicial philosophy, like the Federalist Society or the American Constitution Society. Likewise, student law journals, like the law review at your law school, may maintain a list of past members who clerked and contact information for those former members.

Professors. Finally, don't forget the professors at your law school! They can be a wealth of information about clerking. First, as I have already discussed, many professors clerked after law school, so they can tell you about the process and their own experiences. Second, as prominent members of the local legal community, your professors may have connections to local state and federal judges. I have developed friendships with many of our local judges, and I often hear from them when they are looking for clerks. I strongly encourage you to meet with professors and talk to them about your interest in clerking. Don't be afraid to reach out to a professor that you haven't had for class—most of us are very willing to meet with and assist students.

All of this research on judges and connections can help you develop a list of judges for your clerkship applications. In the next chapter I will discuss building a strong application package.

Short & Happy!

- Honestly evaluate the relative strength of your application to ascertain where you should clerk. Don't be afraid to ask a professor for help with this step.

- Look for "connections" with judges. Connections can be geographic, professional, or shared personal interests.

- There are numerous sources out there for researching judges—don't be afraid to ask your law librarians for help!

CHAPTER 5

HOW Do You Apply?

There's nothing wrong with calling a particular judge's chambers, and saying, "I want to submit a judicial clerk application. What does the judge want?"

~Justice Ruth McGregor[1]

Now that you have thought about where you want to clerk, it is time to start putting together your list of judges and your application materials, which is the focus of this chapter. I will cover pre-application preparation and discuss in detail the application materials that most judges require.

Pre-Application Preparation

Your ability to engage in pre-application preparation will depend largely on when you start thinking about clerking. The sooner you start, the more proactive you can be at the preparatory stage. For example, if your goal is to clerk at the federal appellate level, then your preparation should really start before you matriculate! You should do your best to attend a top-ten law school and secure good grades while at that school. But let's face it, most

---

[1]   Tom R. Arterburn, *The Clerkship Club*, 30 STUDENT LAW. 18, 21 (2001).

students don't plan that far in advance. Because of that, I will give you preparatory steps that you can take while in law school to help you obtain a post-graduation clerkship.

Law School Courses

I'd rather have somebody who's intellectually curious, who spends a lot of time taking hard classes, who has performed well in law school.

~Judge David Stras[2]

One way to develop a strong application is by taking rigorous law school courses that relate to the work that you will do as a clerk. This doesn't mean you can't take that course called "Law and Television"; it just means that your transcript needs to have more substantive courses and fewer "Law and . . ." courses. If you apply to local clerkships, you should also take courses with notoriously difficult professors. The local judges know who the tough professors are. They may have had them in law school!

Here are some courses (roughly listed in order of importance) that can help strengthen your transcript for clerkship applications:

- *Federal Courts*—This course is a must if you want to clerk at the federal level, as it gives you a detailed look at the doctrines controlling the operation of the federal courts. It is also a valuable course for state court clerkships, as many of the doctrines learned in Federal Courts are transferrable to some state systems. Further, the course helps you better understand how the federal and state court systems fit together.

---

[2]   David R. Stras, Diane S. Sykes & James A. Wynn Jr., *Panel Discussion: Judges' Perspectives on Law Clerk Hiring, Utilization, and Influence*, 98 MARQ. L. REV. 441, 447 (2014).

- *Administrative Law*—If you want to clerk for an ALJ, then Administrative Law is a must. But even if you obtain a more general clerkship, you will find yourself reviewing cases from administrative agencies, like immigration cases at the federal level. Understanding the rules governing agencies is important for appellate clerkships. It is also extremely valuable in the practice of law generally.

- *Trial Practice*—If you want to clerk at the trial level, then taking a class focused on trial practice will help you understand the life cycle of a trial and what to expect in the courtroom. For appellate clerkships it will help you understand where things can and do go wrong at trial and how those errors must be preserved for appeal.

- *Appellate Advocacy or Appellate Practice*—Likewise, if you want to clerk at the appellate level, then taking a class in appellate advocacy will help you understand the life cycle of an appeal. You will better understand important concepts like jurisdiction and standards of review. As an added bonus, you will probably have to write one or two appellate briefs, which can serve as a writing sample for your application.

- *Judicial Opinion Writing*—If your law school offers a class on judicial opinion writing, I strongly recommend taking it. Not only will you get writing experience, but the course will approach writing from a judicial perspective. The main audience for most attorney writing is the court—judges and their law clerks. Judges, on the other hand, write for the parties, the attorneys, and the reviewing court. I think both types of writing are best characterized as persuasive, but instead of writing to persuade the court that your client has the right argument, a judge writes to persuade the various audiences that they have reached the correct, reasoned decision. A class in judicial opinion writing, especially one taught by a current or former judge, can help you learn this skill. It can also help you build those valuable connections that I discussed in Chapter 4.

- *Any other writing course*—As a writing professor I am certainly biased, but you should take as many writing courses as you can. Incidentally, based on my research for this book, most judges agree that taking writing classes is valuable. One of the few things that every lawyer does is write! Plus, judicial clerks write even more than the average lawyer. And when a judge hires you for a clerkship, that judge expects you to know how to write, even if you might not be familiar with the specific subject areas that come before the court.

- *Research-focused classes*—Judges also expect you to know how to research. For most law students, the only research-specific instruction they have is in their first-year writing curriculum. That instruction barely scratches the surface of research. I took an advanced research course in law school, which I found to be incredibly useful during both my clerkship and the rest of my career.

- *Subject matter specific classes*—If you are clerking for a court with jurisdiction over a specific subject matter, like some of the ALJ courts, Tribal courts, or international courts, it would behoove you to take a course or two in that specific area—like Environmental Law, Federal Indian Law, or International Human Rights.

Activities & Organizations

You can also bolster your application by participating in law school activities and other organizations. Here are a few examples (in no particular order):

- *Law Review or other law journal work*—Some judges, particularly at the appellate level, require their applicants to have served on a law journal. Some judges require that you serve on the flagship journal at your school—the named law review or law journal—while others value any journal service. Even if a judge doesn't require journal service, it is still widely considered an application booster. This isn't surprising, because a law clerk will review a judge's written work product and check citations, similar to the work that you do on a journal. Many clerks hearken back to their law journal days when faced with tricky citation puzzles, and it is important to show your judge and your future employer—whoever they may be—that you will do your best on the nitty gritty, tedious work, not just the "sexy" writing projects.

- *Federalist Society or American Constitution Society (ACS)*—Federalist Society and ACS have been mentioned elsewhere in this book. They are two of the most prominent ideological (although not expressly political) legal organizations in the country. Membership in either organization can signal to a judge how you believe that legal documents, like the Constitution, should be interpreted. For some judges this matters—a lot. For others it doesn't. You should be able to tell from your judge research if a judge you are applying to cares. Both of these organizations offer tremendous networking opportunities.

- *Federal Bar Association (FBA), American Inns of Court, or the American Bar Association (ABA)*—The FBA, American Inns of Court, and the ABA are prominent non-ideological legal organizations that could bolster your application. The FBA has local chapters across the country. These chapters are made up of federal judges and attorneys who primarily practice in federal court. I am on the board of the local Tucson chapter, and we hold monthly seminars on topics of interest to federal practitioners. We have several local magistrate judges on our board, and we love law student participation. For the past few years, our chapter has held a yearly lawyer/judge/student mixer at the law school. This event is usually well-attended by judges, lawyers, and students. The American Inns of Court has a similar structure. I have former students who participated in the Inns of Court while in law school and had the opportunity to network with judges who were also members. The ABA's divisions are focused on subject matter and not location, so there is a Law Student Division, a Young Lawyers Division, and a Judicial Division, among others.[3] Some judges are very involved in the ABA and would

---

[3]   *ABA Groups*, AM. BAR ASS'N, https://www.americanbar.org/groups/ (last visited Aug. 28, 2022).

look favorably on student participation in the organization while in law school.

- *Other affinity-based student organizations*—If you are applying to a clerkship focused on a specific area of law, then belonging to an affinity organization focusing on that area of law can help your application. For example, you can join an environmental law group if you want to apply for a clerkship with an Environmental Protection Agency ALJ.

- *Skills competitions*—Some judges prize applications from students who participated in skills competitions, like trial advocacy or moot court. This is especially true with judges who participated in skills competitions in law school or who frequently judge these competitions. In some cases, these competitions can also be a way to connect with judges who judge the competitions. Just like with affinity-based organizations, subject-specific competitions give added value to subject-specific clerkships. For example, participating in the National Native American Law Student Association Moot Court competition can connect you to Tribal judges and serve as a strong qualification for a Tribal clerkship. Or participating in the Philip C. Jessup International Law Moot Court Competition can demonstrate your interest in international law and build connections with judges and practitioners worldwide to help you get an international clerkship.

- *Research assistant position*—Any job researching and writing for a professor is a great resume boost. First, it shows a judge that you are experienced doing the very work that you will be doing for the judge—researching and writing on legal issues. And while academic writing is different from judicial writing, you will develop core skills as a research assistant that you will use in a clerkship. These skills include attention to detail, the ability to work independently and collaboratively, and organization. Second, working as a research assistant nearly guarantees you a great letter of recommendation from that professor! And, unlike a regular professor who may only be able to comment on your grade or participation in class, if you have served as a research assistant, that professor can comment in more detail on your written work product and work ethic.

• *Networking opportunities*—Networking opportunities may stem from student organizations or other local or national lawyer organizations. I cannot overstate how important networking opportunities can be to your clerkship applications. They allow you to meet and talk to judges in an informal setting. You can use these connections in your cover letters to judges—"We met at the Federal Bar Association reception at the law school last year. I enjoyed talking to you about your time in the U.S. Attorney's Office." Who knows, your informal conversations at these events may turn into an internship offer, which could open the door to a clerkship! When I was a 1L, I attended a lunch for a student organization and ended up sitting next to a judge who was our speaker. The fact that I shared a geographic connection and alma mater with the judge prompted him to offer me a summer internship. Because that judge didn't hire his interns as clerks, I declined (I really wanted to clerk for him). Meeting judges in an informal setting can also help demystify judges as people. Interviewing for a clerkship can be quite intimidating. If you have never talked one-on-one with a judge, the situation becomes even more intimidating. But judges are regular people too. They have lives and interests outside of the law. Trust me—I see what my judge friends post on social media. Talking to judges at networking events can help ease you into the types of conversations that you will have with judges once you interview for clerkships.

Externships/Internships/Summer Jobs

Back in the (prehistoric) days of the federal clerkship hiring plan in place when I applied for clerkships, the 2L summer job was key to clerkship plans. Applications were due at the end of the 2L summer, so we could focus on getting a great letter of recommendation from our 2L summer employers. And, if we were lucky, we would also work for attorneys who clerked and who were willing to personally contact judges to recommend us. Now that applications for federal clerkships and many state clerkships are due at the start of the 2L summer, the 2L job has lost its importance for clerkship purposes, unless you are looking at a clerkship with a later application deadline.

Despite this diminishing of the 2L summer experience, your 1L summer job and a 2L semester internship or externship can still help strengthen your application materials, especially if they result in a strong letter of recommendation or demonstrate work similar to what you would do as a clerk. If you start thinking about clerkships during your 1L year, then obtaining a good 1L summer job and a fall

2L internship should be high on your law school priority list. In particular, interning or externing for a judge during your 1L summer or at the start of your 2L year can be especially helpful for recommendation and connection purposes. And although many judges have policies against writing letters of recommendation, they are often willing to serve as references and speak directly to other judges on your behalf.

Researching Judges

One of the most important pre-application preparatory things that you can do is start researching judges. In Chapter 4, I discuss questions that you should ask as you develop your judge application list. I also discuss key sources for researching judges.

You should create a spreadsheet to organize your judge research. Important information for the spreadsheet would be:

- Judge's name;

- Court;

- Application deadline;

- Application method (email or paper) and relevant address(es);

- Any connections you share with the judge (see Chapter 4); and

- Why you are applying to this judge.

There might be other information that you could include in the spreadsheet depending on your circumstances. See the next page for a sample spreadsheet.

Judge	Court	Connections	Key Judicial Opinions	Publications	Interests	Notes

Developing this spreadsheet early in your clerkship journey is an excellent strategy. I recommend starting during your 1L summer, after you receive your spring semester grades and before you get crazy busy as a 2L. If you are reading this as a 2L or 3L student, start as soon as you finish reading this book! Once you have your base spreadsheet, you can keep it updated as new judges are appointed, confirmed, or elected, which brings me to my penultimate preparation point.

Don't Forget the Recent Appointees!

Your judge list should not remain static because the bench does not remain static. In the federal system judges can take senior status or fully retire at any time of the year, and new judges are nominated and confirmed for these positions. This is also true on most state benches, even for courts that are elected. In those elected-jurisdictions, the governor may be able to appoint someone to a vacancy prior to an election.

New judges provide a unique opportunity for graduates who are looking to use a clerkship as a career or location shift, especially if the opening occurs during the academic year. For 3Ls who might have missed the traditional hiring cycle for a court, you should also be watching for new judges. In some instances, those judges will hire short-term clerks with prior clerking experience as they get acclimated to their position, while at the same time looking for term clerks to start during the "normal" clerkship cycle.

Figure out the Timing

As I have discussed elsewhere, the timing of clerkship applications can be tricky. Some judges and courts make their application deadlines very clear—often on a dedicated court webpage for clerkships or in the OSCAR system. But for other judges, you will need to do some work to figure out the timing. Timing, for some clerkships, can vary not just by court but also by judge.

If your selected judges fall into the "unclear timing" category, you will need to call or email chambers to ask about application deadlines, required materials, and application delivery method (mail or email). Fortunately, most chambers expect to receive these questions and are happy to supply you with the information.

Application Materials

> *The clerkship application process should feel like a full-time job—don't skimp on it.*
>
> ~Judge Willie J. Epps, Jr.[4]

Most clerkship applications are made up of the following components:

- Legal resume. This should highlight your law school credentials, including any awards (such as in skills competitions or top grades in classes). It should also include membership in student organizations, including any leadership roles. It should describe your law-related employment history, including research assistant positions, internships, externships, and summer jobs. It should also include significant pre-law school employment, for example if you had a break between your undergraduate degree and law school.

- Transcript. Include your law school transcript. Some judges may also want an undergraduate transcript,

---

[4]   Willie J. Epps Jr. & Jonathan M. Warren, *The Who, What, When, Where, Why, and How of Clerking, as Told by a Federal Judge and His Former Law Clerk*, 90 UMKC L. REV. 295, 311 (2021).

so be sure to request a few copies from your undergrad institution if you don't have one handy.

- Cover letter. I will discuss the cover letter in more detail later, but this one-page letter should introduce you to the judge and explain what you are applying for and why.

- Writing sample. I will also discuss the writing sample later. In general, the writing sample should be ten to fifteen pages doubled-spaced, unless the job posting says otherwise. It should be a piece of legal writing that represents your own work (meaning it hasn't been heavily edited by someone else). "Heavily edited" will mean different things to different people. Generally, a writing sample that has been proofread for typos and clarity by another person is fine.

- Letters of recommendation. Most judges ask for three letters of recommendation. I will discuss these letters in more detail later in this chapter.

Although judges generally require the same application documents, they weigh the relative value of these documents differently. For example, I have heard judges say that they rely most heavily on letters of recommendation, while other judges say the letters count very little in their analysis. This means that as an applicant, you need to treat every piece of the application package as the most important piece.

Some judges also require the top applicants to complete a writing test. Sometimes this will be during the interview; other times you will have to do a self-monitored timed test at home. The writing prompt may be similar to a law school exam question, and both your writing and Bluebooking are scrutinized. Some clerks who crush their in-person interviews bomb a timed writing test. If you have any concerns about completing this type of exercise, you should practice.[5]

One final note about applications. Many judges use their law clerks to cull applications. This is especially true at the federal appellate level, where judges who use OSCAR can get hundreds of applications. This means that you don't need to just impress the judge with your application—you also need to stand out to the clerks. Following the tips in this chapter will help with that difficult endeavor.

Who Should Write Your Letters of Recommendation?

I also look at the recommendation letter; if it merely discusses an individual's good grades, I learn nothing about the actual character or work ethic of that person. A professor who knows you well can speak to your character and work ethic, or even explain what a certain grade means at a particular school.

~Judge Catharina Haynes[6]

When I talk to students about letters of recommendation, I love to tell the following story. When I was applying for clerkships, I thought I should get the most prestigious professors at my school to write me letters. I am assuming someone told me to do this, but I can't recall. So, I went to one of my professors who was extremely well-known and asked him to write me a letter. He said that he would be happy to write me a letter, but all it would say was that I got a mediocre grade in his class, and I didn't participate in class

---

[5]   Incidentally, one of the best ways to practice your legal writing is to use sample bar exam questions. With limited time, try to kill two birds with one stone!

[6]   JUDICIAL CLERKSHIP FORUM: A CONVERSATION WITH 12 JUDGES, AMERICAN BAR ASSOCIATION JUDICIAL DIVISION LAWYERS CONFERENCE 16 (2015).

discussions. I am sure that he said it much more nicely than that, but you get the idea. He suggested I ask people who knew me better (and had better things to say) to write letters for me. This was *very* sound advice, which I followed. Here is the moral of that story: a good letter from someone who knows you well is worth far more than a mediocre or poor letter from someone "famous."

What makes a letter good? A good letter reflects the skills and abilities that would make you a good clerk. What are these skills and abilities? Here is a list of things that I like to mention, when applicable, in my letters:

- Strong writing skills;

- Strong research skills;

- Strong analytical skills;

- Strong academic skills;

- Proactive;

- Organized;

- Ethical/honest/trustworthy;

- Well-liked or -trusted in the law school community (i.e.—peers respect the applicant);

- Strong interpersonal skills (good fit for a chambers environment); and

- Some sort of comparative analysis with past students. For example, "James is the best student I have taught in my decade in academia." Or, "In my opinion, as a former federal appellate clerk and professor for over seven years, you could not pick a better clerk than Vera."

For students who are strong applicants, my letters of recommendation are typically two pages long. If I know the judge personally or professionally, I may also say something about the student's personality vis-à-vis the judge's, and how they would work well together in a small chambers environment.

If these are the attributes of a good letter of recommendation, who should write your letters? You should ask professors and legal employers who can comment honestly on these aspects of your character and work product.

You may hear from a career services office or a professor that only tenured or tenure-track doctrinal professors should write your letters. Without getting into the politics of academic status (a very messy topic), I will just say that is bad advice (except perhaps for judges who are recovering academics). If you got a good grade in a legal writing class and developed a good relationship with your legal writing professor, ask that professor to write a letter. The same is true for a clinical or skills class or an independent study professor. From my experience teaching both doctrinal and skills classes, I can better opine on a student's suitability for a clerkship if I have taught that student in Appellate Advocacy versus Constitutional Law.

If you are submitting three letters of recommendation, at least one letter should be from a faculty member at your law school and at least one letter should be from an employer or internship supervisor. The third letter could be from either a professor or employer.

If possible, you should request letters from professors and employers a month in advance. I require students to give me at least two weeks' notice. Please keep in mind that most letter requests come in May, which is a busy grading time for faculty. Be prepared to provide your recommenders with your resume and transcript, as well as a list of judges you are applying to. For me this list is important—I will often reach out to the judges that I know personally. And, it is always good form to send a thank you note to your recommenders. You should also keep them up to date on your clerkship search.

One final note about letters of recommendation. Popular professors might be asked by multiple students for letters of recommendation. This can get tricky if the students are all applying for the same clerkships. I have heard from judges that they dislike getting five or six letters from the same professor recommending different students for a position. If you are an applicant, consider nicely asking your recommenders if they are writing multiple letters. If you are a professor, keep this in mind if you are asked to write multiple letters to the same judge. The few times I have found myself in this position, I reach out to the judge personally to discuss the applicants.

What Should You Use for a Writing Sample?

Most clerkship writing samples should be under fifteen pages, unless otherwise noted in the job posting. And unless a judge says otherwise, your writing sample should, to the best of your ability, be a document that mirrors the style of writing that you might do for a judge. Thus, a memorandum on a legal question, a motion or appellate brief, or a judicial opinion from an opinion-writing class are generally better writing samples than student law review notes. You should only use a student note as a writing sample if (1) you think that it would particularly interest a certain judge, such as something related to one of the judge's past opinions or practice areas; (2) if the note was prominently published; (3) or if you don't have a strong practice-oriented writing sample.

Generally, judges expect your writing sample to represent your own work—meaning that it hasn't been heavily edited by anyone else. You should include a cover page for your writing sample that explains the document and notes any editing that occurred. For example:

The following writing sample is from a brief that I wrote for Advanced Legal Writing, which I took during the Fall 2022 semester. I am including the issue presented for issue one, the statement of the case, and my discussion of issue one, which addresses the circuit split over whether reasonable suspicion is required for a forensic search of a cell phone at a border crossing. This excerpt is solely my own work, although I received general feedback on a draft outline from my professor.

A few other points to consider on the writing sample. First, if possible, your writing sample should not be from your first year in law school, even if you got a good grade. This is because your legal writing skills should develop over your three years in law school through advanced writing classes and legal employment or internship experiences. Does this mean you should sign up for an advanced writing class as a 2L? Yes, it does. View it as an opportunity to develop a writing sample. If you don't, please be sure to focus on getting a writing sample from your 1L summer job or a 2L internship. Second, if you want to use a writing sample from a job or an internship, you must get permission from your supervisor to use the writing sample. You may also need to redact client information from the document.

How Do You Write a Cover Letter?

In my chambers, my law clerks take a substantial hand in selecting their following law clerks. They do all the initial screening. What I usually get is about 20 to 15

> *applications that I'll screen myself and then determine*
> *to interview maybe eight to 10 of those finalists.*

~Judge Michael S. Kanne[7]

Remember how I said earlier that clerks often cull applications for judges? This is, in part, because the benefits of technology have allowed students to easily apply to hundreds of clerkships at a time. Back in the prehistoric time when I applied for clerkships, judges required paper applications. That means X number of cover letters, writing samples, and letters of recommendation. And the postage! I was fortunate—my law school played a pivotal role in collecting my letters of recommendation, duplicating my materials, and mailing them out. I have friends who were not so lucky.

Now, for most applications, you either email materials to a chambers or upload them on OSCAR. This could allow a student to apply to every open clerkship position with little added effort. This "shotgun" approach might sound like a good idea (i.e., the more places I apply, the more likely I am to get a clerkship). But guess what, it isn't. You are better off spending your time developing a strong, carefully thought-out judge list and personalizing cover letters for each of these judges.

Now, before you get too stressed out, personalizing cover letters doesn't mean starting from scratch each time. You should create a shell or a template to use for your applications then fill in the necessary information and personalize it for the specific judge.

Your cover letter should not exceed one page and should include the following information:

The first paragraph is an introduction to who you are, what position you are applying for, and why. For example:

---

[7]   Kevin Allen, *Seventh Circuit judges share advice, insights on clerkships*, UNIVERSITY OF NOTRE DAME SCHOOL OF LAW (Feb. 5, 2020), https://law.nd.edu/news-events/news/seventh-circuit-judges-clerkships-panel/.

- Who you are—"I am a rising third-year law student at the University of Arizona James E. Rogers College of Law." Mentioning your school will help draw attention to school-related connections you might have with the judge.

- What you are applying for—"I am applying for a one-year clerkship in your chambers starting in August 2026."

- The "why" would cover any especially important connections you want to highlight that explain why you are applying to this particular judge. Here are a few examples:

  - Geographic: "As a native Arizonan who plans to practice in state court, I am particularly interested in clerking for a state court judge in Arizona."

  - School: "I too attended Willamette University for college, although I left Oregon for law school. I would like to return to Oregon to clerk and ultimately practice law."

  - Career-oriented: "Following my clerkship, I plan to apply for DOJ Honors and work in a U.S. Attorney's Office. I am especially interested in clerking for you given your similar career path."

  - Personal: "Professor Dysart recommended that I apply to you. I have enclosed a letter of recommendation from her." This is only useful to include if the judge will know the personal connection. Because the judge's clerks are probably taking the first or second stab at culling applications, you could even write something like, "Your law school moot court partner, Professor Tessa (Platt) Dysart recommended that I apply to you."

- This could also include a personal connection that you developed with a judge: "We met last year at the Federal Bar Association mixer and discussed my interest in being a public defender after law school. I appreciated that conversation and your advice."

The next two paragraphs should discuss further reasons why you want to clerk for that judge and highlight your qualifications for the job. This qualifications section should be tailored to the specific type of court. In discussing your qualifications, please be sure to not simply repeat information from your resume. You can highlight and further develop items from your resume, but just listing your previous experience is not helpful.

For example, if you are applying for a trial level clerkship you should expound upon any trial work on your resume or that you will do during your 2L summer. Similarly, if you are applying for an appellate clerkship and you assisted in writing five appellate briefs during an internship with the state attorney general's office, you might mention that fact. I have one friend who interned for a federal judge while in law school. Although she was not permitted to use opinions that she helped draft as writing samples, her judge allowed her to cite them in her cover letter. This is a great example on how to build on your resume and experience in a cover letter. American University Washington College of Law puts it nicely in their advice on cover letters: "Remember that the function of a clerkship cover letter is to highlight certain aspects of your resume that demonstrate your qualifications for the clerkship, not to summarize your resume. Be sure to discuss how you will benefit the judge, not just how the clerkship will benefit you."[8]

The final paragraph of the letter should explain what application materials you have included, how to reach you for interviews or other information, and a list of people who have agreed to serve as references but haven't written a letter. This final list would include any judicial references.

Although it should go without saying, please proofread your letter for typos (and ask a few trusted friends to proofread it too). Be sure that you have the judge's name and title correct, including any initials and suffixes. Don't inadvertently promote a federal appellate judge to the state (or U.S.) supreme court (judge v. justice) or neglect to note if a judge is the chief judge or justice of a jurisdiction. These little things matter, especially to the clerks, who will be unreasonably picky because they are wading through stacks of applications like yours. Care for the details will demonstrate your attention to detail, or lack thereof.

The Extra Boost

> *[T]he people I've hired have tended to be people whose recommenders have called me.*
>
> ~Judge David Stras[9]
>
> *In deciding which applicants to interview, the judge relies primarily on recommendations by law professors whom he knows personally and trusts, or on oral follow-ups to written recommendations from law professors he doesn't know, because it is widely believed by judges that written recommendations are often exaggerated but*

---

[8] *Application Process: Cover Letters*, AM. UNIV. WASH. COLL. OF L., https://www.wcl.american.edu/career/student/sectors/judicial/application/cover/ (last visited Aug. 28, 2022).

[9] Stras et al., *supra* note 2, at 447.

that the recommender will level with the judge over the phone.

~Judge Richard Posner[10]

The last part of your application materials comes in the form of what I call an "extra boost." This is a phone call, text message, Facebook message, email, or the like from one of your references or recommenders to the judge. Not every application or every candidate will get this extra boost, but if you think one of your references or recommenders will do this, don't be afraid to ask.

To the professors reading this book—be willing to put in the extra boost. When I personally contact a judge, I am very honest. I have been asked in the past to contact judges, and I will tell the judge when we talk, "I don't think that this student is a great fit for your chambers for X, Y, Z reason." My relationship with the judge and any future possibility of placing clerks with that judge is too important to risk on a bad clerkship fit. The judges I reach out to personally are both judges that were my classmates in law school and judges that I have met more recently as an academic. I have also reached out to career clerks to talk to them about applicants. Both judges and clerks have contacted me to discuss applicants.

For applicants who don't have anyone to give this extra boost, let me reassure you that it doesn't always make the difference—sometimes to my surprise! Ultimately, your success as an applicant depends on the final part of the application process—the interview.

The Interview

When I'm interviewing someone, I'm just having a conversation with them. I'm talking to them because I'm trying to get a feel for how do they interact

---

[10] Mitu Gulati & Richard A. Posner, *The Management of Staff by Federal Court of Appeals Judges*, 69 VAND. L. REV. 479, 483 (2016).

professionally with people, how are they going to interact with the attorneys.

~Judge Francisco Dominguez[11]

I am tempted to call the interview the most important part of the application process, although usually your application gets you to the interview. Assuming an applicant has the basic qualifications for a clerkship with a particular judge, then I think you can fairly call the interview the most important step in the process. When I talk to students who interviewed for a clerkship and didn't get the position, I try to reassure them they probably didn't do anything "wrong" in the interview; they just weren't a great fit for that judge, or someone else was an even better fit. Fit is a part of the application that is very difficult to manipulate, but very important for most hiring judges.

You can try to apply to judges who you think would be a great fit, but you can't control that someone else might be applying who is an even better fit. This means that you need to do all that you can to prepare for the interview and interview well, but you also need to understand that much of the process, at this point, is out of your control. As frustrating as this is, it should take a bit of pressure off you so you can walk into the interview and be yourself—the best, most polished version of yourself.

Preparing for the Interview

Preparing for the interview includes a good measure of self-reflection and research about the judge and the court. Let's talk first about the self-reflection. Before you attend the interview, you should have good answers to the following questions:

1.   Why do you want to clerk (in general)?

---

[11]   Njcourts, *Judicial Clerkship Program Webinar*, YOUTUBE, 54:56-55:09 (July 7, 2020), https://www.youtube.com/watch?v=pM5VQcBhh2s.

2.   Why do you want to clerk for me?

3.   Why do you want to clerk in this jurisdiction/
      state/city?

4.   What do you want to do with your legal career?

5.   How does a clerkship fit into your overall career
      goals?

If you are applying to both trial and appellate clerkships, you might have different standard answers for questions 1, 3, 4, and 5. Your answer for question 2 should, naturally, be personalized to the specific judge.

Other possible self-reflection questions include:[12]

6.   Why did you go to law school?

7.   Tell me about yourself. Or, tell me about your
      interest in ___. (Here a judge would fill in an interest
      that you talk about in your application materials).

8.   What do you like to do in your free time?

9.   What books have you recently read? (Note—they
      aren't asking about your textbooks, so try to read
      something interesting over your 1L summer. I
      recommend a great presidential biography, like Ron
      Chernow's *Grant* or David McCullough's *John Adams*
      or an epic fiction novel, like *Dune* or *Atlas Shrugged*.
      One of my friends suggested something by Malcolm
      Gladwell.)

10.   Tell me about your writing sample.

---

[12]   Many of these questions were taken from a New York University School of Law resource, *Interview Tips and Other Important Information*, N.Y. UNIV. SCH. OF L., http://www.law.nyu.edu/sites/default/files/upload_documents/Interview%20Tips%20%26%20FAQ.pdf (last visited Aug. 28, 2022), and from a University of Wisconsin Law School resource, *Sample Clerkship Interview Questions*, UNIV. OF WIS.-MADISON L. SCH., https://law.wisc.edu/career/interviewquestions.html (last visited Aug. 28, 2022).

11. Do you like XYZ law school? What is your favorite class? What is your least favorite class?

12. Who is your favorite Supreme Court justice and why? (Think of both a current and a historical answer in case the question is modified in some form.)

13. What justice's judicial philosophy is most appealing to you and why?

14. What other clerkships are you applying to?

15. What are your thoughts on *stare decisis*? Or precedent? Or states' rights? Or the administrative state?

16. How do you describe your work style? Or, how do you describe your writing style?

17. Tell me about your summer experience at the Attorney General's office.

18. Have you ever faced a difficult ethical dilemma? How did you handle it?

19. How do you manage multiple competing projects?

Your answers to this second set of questions can largely remain the same across courts. You might pull in connection information with the judge in answering some of the questions, for example by highlighting that you are both Eagle Scouts or played collegiate water polo or like to surf.

Next, you need to research the judge and the court that the judge sits on. If you are applying to a federal judge, look carefully at the sources discussed in Chapter 4, especially the *Almanac of the Federal Judiciary*. Know the judge's reputation among lawyers, key judicial opinions, publications, and other honors or interests. Read the judge's recent and noteworthy opinions and the judge's publications. I also recommend reviewing the judge's Senate

Questionnaire and hearing transcript, especially if the judge's confirmation hearing was relatively recent. You should also conduct a news and internet search on the judge. You probably want to know what the popular press is saying about them.

You might get substantive questions from the judge based on the judge's past precedents. Be prepared to answer the following questions:

20. Have you read any of my opinions? Which ones?

21. What do you think of my opinion in *Smith v. Jones*?

22. What do you think of my court's decision to hear *Smith v. Jones* en banc?

23. I see that you got the top grade in state constitutional law. I have written extensively on that topic. What did you think of my recent article in the Arizona Bar Journal on the importance of state privacy amendments?

See if any former students from your school clerked for that judge. If they are willing, set up a video call or in-person meeting to talk to them about their experience. If you are involved in a national organization that interfaces with that judge, see if someone at the national organization will talk with you about the judge.

You also need to know how the court operates. For example, in Arizona, the intermediate appellate court does not hear direct appeals from death penalty cases.[13] So, if you tell an Arizona intermediate appellate judge that you want to clerk to get experience on death penalty cases, that judge will likely tell you that you should have applied to clerk on the state supreme court instead. You should know, for example, how often and where an

---

[13]   There are some exceptions, but they aren't relevant to my point.

appellate court hears oral argument. You should know what types of cases traditionally come before that court. All of that information should be easy to find online, if you take the time to look.

You should also know a bit about the location of the judge's chambers. For example, if you are attending law school in an urban environment, are you prepared to clerk for a judge with chambers in a very rural part of a state? Judges want to know you will be a positive addition to chambers and enjoy the place they call home. Career clerks may also ask this question if they are looking for people to join their weekend frisbee games or other after-hours activities. This type of question came up in one of my clerkship interviews. Luckily, I had grown up in a rural area and could honestly say that I preferred that lifestyle.

Finally, be prepared with questions for the judge and clerk. These questions should demonstrate that you have done research about the court and the judge and that you are genuinely interested in the work they do. For example, you can ask clerks what they like most about their job or living in that particular city. For judges, ask them how being a judge compares to their previous employment. Or perhaps ask about the judge's clerkship experience.

Scheduling the Interview

> *I also think it's really important for applicants to make sure that they feel like they have a good rapport with the judge and the judge's staff as well . . . .*

~Judge Aimee Belgard[14]

You may be surprised to hear that your clerkship interview starts the moment you answer the phone call (or return the phone call) inviting you to interview. When talking to chambers staff about

---

[14] Njcourts, *Judicial Clerkship Program Webinar*, YouTube, 49:54-50:04 (July 7, 2020), https://www.youtube.com/watch?v=pM5VQcBhh2s.

scheduling your interview, you should express enthusiasm to interview, even if the judge isn't at the top of your list. This is because you should *only* apply to judges that you are willing to clerk for, absent something abnormal happening in an interview.

Under the current federal hiring plan, federal judges who follow the plan can call you and start scheduling interviews the day after they receive applications. They are not supposed to give any "exploding offers" during the interview. An exploding offer is one that an applicant must accept on the spot. Rather, judges are supposed to give applicants 48 hours to respond to any offers. Other courts might have similar rules. Be sure you know any relevant rules and timelines before the interview requests start.

Despite the 48 hour wait, the federal system still puts applicants in a tricky spot. For example, you might prefer to clerk for a federal appellate judge, but the first call that you receive is from a federal district court chambers. You will have to decide if it is worth the risk to delay scheduling interviews. One tactic would be to not answer your phone for the first hour or so that morning. You can then return calls in order of priority. This is good advice if you think you are an extremely competitive candidate. If you aren't, I would urge you to not delay in scheduling interviews. You can always "stack" clerkships to get both a trial and appellate experience. I will discuss stacking clerkships in more detail in Chapter 6.

A few more points about interview scheduling. First, you are responsible for your travel costs. Sorry. Check with your career services office or dean to see if your law school offers financial assistance. Second, although some judges will allow you to interview via video conferencing, you should try to interview in person unless *all* the other applicants are doing video interviews. Post-COVID, more judges are using video conferencing software for interviews. This is especially helpful for judges in remote locations, especially given the short interview timeline under the federal hiring plan. But, given how important "fit" is for clerkships, you really want to try and appear in person to wow the judge and the chambers staff with your winning personality. And some judges will require in-person interviews without exceptions.

The Actual Interview

> *The interviews themselves are rarely substantive in the sense of the judge's testing the applicant's legal knowledge or analytical skills. Rather the focus is on seeing whether the applicant will "fit" into the culture of the office.*

~Judge Richard Posner[15]

You might think that you are just interviewing with the judge, but you are actually interviewing with the judge's judicial assistant and the judge's clerks (especially if there is a career clerk) too. Basically, you are interviewing with anyone and everyone you interact with at the judge's chambers or courthouse or, if you have a video interview, anyone on or off screen who helps set up and conduct the interview.

One of the most important people in a judge's chambers is the judicial assistant, or JA. Most JA's stay with one judge for the entirety of either their career or the judge's career. If a judge is elevated from the trial to the appellate bench or the state to the federal bench, the judge often brings along their JA. And many judges who enter from a law firm will bring their favorite legal assistant to work for them on the bench. The JA is a gatekeeper to the judge and keeps the judge organized. The JA knows everything that is going on professionally with the judge, and probably most of

---

[15] Mitu Gulati & Richard A. Posner, *The Management of Staff by Federal Court of Appeals Judges*, 69 VAND. L. REV. 479, 483 (2016).

what is going on personally too. This close relationship leads judges to be fiercely protective of their JAs. There are hundreds of law school graduates who could do the work of a law clerk. There is only one JA. If you are rude to the JA, you will not get a clerkship. It does not matter how brilliant you are. I can't think of a single judge who would pick a law clerk over a JA's or career clerk's objection. While you won't formally interview with the JA, you will interact with them over email and during an in-person interview. They will likely be the first person you meet when you step into chambers. Sometimes JAs and career clerks will even purposely delay the beginning of an interview a few minutes to see how you handle the wait and choose to interact with the JA. Always treat them with kindness and respect.

I think that some of this reasoning also extends to other figures in the courthouse. For judges who work in a courthouse building, they interact frequently with security staff. If you are rude while going through security, reports of that interaction will probably make it to the judge (maybe even before you get to the judge's chambers) and will reflect poorly on your application. The same is true if you are rude to IT staff when setting up a video interview. Having chatted with numerous judges over video conferencing during COVID, I know how much they rely on their IT staff! The best course of action is quite simple—be nice to everyone. I was once asking my four-year-old if he knew what I taught as a professor. He said, "You teach people to be nice to each other and not take away toys." In a sense he is at least half right—being nice goes a long way in the practice of law, in clerkship interviews, and in life. Be nice.

Many judges do have clerkship applicants formally interview with their clerks. This is an important part of the process. The clerks are often gauging "fit"—will you fit into the chambers environment? This is especially true if there is a career clerk on staff. The clerks want to know if, among other things, you will be a fun person to eat lunch with every workday for a year. You might think that I am joking—I'm not. During my clerkship year not only did we eat lunch together frequently, we also drove together to Richmond for oral argument—a six hour ride. This doesn't mean that you shouldn't be prepared for substantive questions from the clerks and the judge, but just know that more than your answers to substantive questions is being evaluated in a clerkship interview. Be honest about the books you read and the hobbies you enjoy. It might cost you a clerkship—one of my friends "failed" an interview for having never watched an episode of *The Walking Dead*—but clerks (and the JA if they join this part of the interview) will see right through you if you are trying to come off as smarter or fancier than you are. Always be honest and try to maintain a pleasant, open demeanor during the entire interview process.

One other interview tip—plan on arriving early. You never know what might happen regarding traffic, parking, the weather, or courthouse security. Plan to be at your interview with plenty of time to spare. If you are too early you can always walk around the building or the block to work off any nervous energy.

The Virtual Interview

If you do have to interview virtually, here are a few tips for a successful virtual interview.

- See if you can test the software in advance with someone from the judge's chambers or IT department, especially if it isn't software that you commonly use. You should also plan on "arriving" to your virtual interview early, logging in at least ten minutes before it starts.

- Do the interview in a location with a neutral background. I recommend not using a virtual background, since you run the risk of your arm or head seeming to disappear. Rather, pick a place with a neutral-colored wall, bookshelf, or art piece. Don't have your back to a window, as this will make your face harder to see. If your living quarters doesn't offer a quiet place with a neutral background, check with the career services office at your law school to see if you can use their conference room or another room on campus. If you are using a location in your home, please be sure that there is nothing unseemly or controversial in the background. What book titles are visible on your bookshelf? What pictures? What posters?

- Pick a quiet location. If you are using a room on campus or if you have roommates, put a note on the door to alert others that you are interviewing. Sequester any pets that might intrude on your interview.

- If you are at home, minimize internet usage in your house during the interview. Ask your roommates or spouse to pause any gaming or streaming for the time of your interview. You want all the internet resources going into a high-quality video stream. You might even have a back-up device ready if your computer or laptop fails.

- Try your best to look at the camera on your device, not at the screen. If possible, find a way to position your camera so that you can look at both the camera and the screen at the same time. This helps mimic eye contact—you want the judge and clerks to feel like you are looking at them, not at another screen. Practice this with friends or family before your interview. You might even record yourself to see how you look.

- During the interview close all other applications on your computer and silence your phone (or put it in another room altogether). You do not need anything distracting you! You also don't want email sound notifications on your computer interrupting your conversation with the judge.

- Check your lighting in advance and at the same time of day as your interview. In general, you appear best with front lighting, not back lighting.

- Dress professionally from head to toe. Even if you plan on remaining seated during the interview, you never know what might happen (I say this from experience).

Send a Thank You!

Shortly after your interview be sure to drop a nice thank you note into the mail. Consider sending notes to everyone you meet— the JA, the clerks, and the judge. Be sure that the notes are personalized to your experiences with the receiver. For example, you could thank the JA for scheduling the interview and note that you appreciated talking to them about their experiences working for the judge.

You can also email thank you notes, but there is something really special about getting a thank you card in the mail.

The Offer

The prevailing wisdom is that if a judge offers you a clerkship you accept it. This is generally sound advice. As I discussed earlier, you should not apply to clerk for a judge that you would not accept an offer from, barring something unusual happening during the interview process.

However, I do think that there are situations where you can ask the judge for time to think about the offer or complete other scheduled interviews. But understand, you do this at your peril—the judge might rescind the offer or be offended. And the subsequent interviews might not yield offers. If this all sounds tricky to navigate—it is. As I said earlier, for judges who follow the federal hiring plan, they should give you 48 hours to consider an offer. This should give you time to complete interviews already scheduled for that same day.

Consider this example. Let's say you interview with Judge Alvarez on Monday at 9 am, and Judge Alvarez offers you a clerkship at the conclusion of the interview. But, you have an interview with Judge Bonita lined up for later that day at 1 pm, and you prefer to work for Judge Bonita. I think that it is appropriate to keep your interview with Judge Bonita and make your decision after that interview. You need to communicate this respectfully to Judge Alvarez. I wouldn't say, "I prefer to work for Judge Bonita." Rather, I would say, "My interview with Judge Bonita is later this afternoon, and I think that it is too late to cancel that interview." Likewise, when you interview with Judge Bonita, you need to inform them that you have an offer from Judge Alvarez that you need to respond to by Tuesday afternoon, but that your first choice would be to clerk for Judge Bonita because of Judge Bonita's work as a water law attorney. Be careful how you express preferences—judges talk to each other, even judges on different courts.

But, if you have interviews with Judges Chavez, Davis, and Eller on Tuesday and Wednesday, I would cancel those interviews. If you don't have any other interviews lined up, I would accept the first offer that you receive. If it is a trial clerkship and you want an appellate clerkship, you can always stack clerkships.

Navigating offers is one place where it can help to talk to a trusted advisor, like a professor or the career services office. If a professor or former employer personally recommended you to a judge, I especially encourage you talk to that person about navigating offers, since your decision will reflect not just on you but also on the person who personally recommended you.

Now that you have your offer in hand, let's discuss making the most of your clerkship year!

Short & Happy!

- You can strengthen your clerkship application by taking the right classes and participating in the right activities.
- Take the time to carefully put together your clerkship application materials, including tailoring cover letters.
- Seek out letters of recommendation from professors and employers who can speak to your work ethic and abilities.
- Be nice to *everyone* at your interview.

CHAPTER 6

The Clerkship Year and Beyond

Not only will you learn a lot from the judge by virtue of working closely with the judge for the year, but then that judge also becomes your advocate for life. The judges for whom I clerked became my mentors. They went to bat for me when I was looking for jobs, and they gave me advice about jobs.

~Justice Amy Coney Barrett[1]

Congratulations, you did it! You secured a clerkship and can now look forward to the best job ever. But with a clerkship comes great responsibility—the responsibility to make the most of your clerkship year, the responsibility to act ethically both during and after your clerkship, and the responsibility to give back to your law school community. You also have the responsibility to find a post-clerkship job.

---

[1] Kevin Allen, *Seventh Circuit judges share advice, insights on clerkships*, UNIVERSITY OF NOTRE DAME SCHOOL OF LAW (Feb. 5, 2020), https://law.nd.edu/news-events/news/seventh-circuit-judges-clerkships-panel/.

Making the Most of Your Clerkship Year

Much like I encourage law students to make the most of their law school experience by networking and attending cool events on campus, you should make the most of your clerkship year by doing the same.

First, be intentional about getting to know your judge, co-clerks, and the other chambers staff. Go to lunch with them. If they don't initiate a request, then you plan something. Just think, you could be that term's social director! If you clerk on a court that travels for oral argument, ask to travel with the judge. This travel can be taxing if you have family obligations, but trust me, traveling for court is when you really get to know your judge and co-clerks!

Second, get to know the other judges, clerks, and court staff. If the court plans a welcome dinner or other event for clerks, attend it. I still recall the welcome dinner when I clerked. It was a great opportunity to meet other judges in a less formal setting. If the court plans regular CLEs or other gatherings for clerks and court staff—attend those too. When I was clerking, we frequently went to lunch during oral argument week with the clerks whose judges were sitting with our judge. There was one occasion when nearly every judge and clerk on the court ended up eating lunch at the same time in the same sandwich shop across the street from the courthouse. My judge also planned a dinner for us with another judge's chambers. That dinner helped me build a friendship with one of that judge's clerks, who is now a judge.

Third, take time to network with national legal organizations, with your judge's permission of course. If it interests you, and your judge approves, attend national or regional conferences for legal organizations—like the Federalist Society's National Lawyers Convention, the American Constitution Society's National Conference, or ABA conferences.

Fourth, take a little time for yourself. I came to my clerkship from an intense three years in law school that, as a first-generation law student from a rural area of Oregon, was an eye-opening culture shock. I needed a break. And while I did all the things I suggest above, I also took time for self-care. I exercised. I made friends. It was wonderful.

Know Your Ethical Limitations as a Clerk

The clerk is really an extension of the judge. I tell my clerks that they've got one job—and they realize it when they come in—that job is to make the judge look good. Wherever they go for the rest of their lives, they will be identified in connection with their judge. If you don't fulfill your duty to your fellow clerks and to your chambers of making your judge look good, you're hurting yourself. It's more than just a family. It's a connected, professional relationship that you develop.

~Judge James Wynn[2]

As a clerk you are subject to ethical rules. The specific rules will vary based on jurisdiction, but the general principles are the same. These rules are in place to avoid any appearance of impropriety or undue influence and to protect the integrity of the judicial system. Beyond the specific ethical rules in place in your jurisdiction, your judge may require you to follow other restrictions.[3]

---

[2]   David R. Stras, Diane S. Sykes & James A. Wynn Jr., *Panel Discussion: Judges' Perspectives on Law Clerk Hiring, Utilization, and Influence*, 98 Marq. L. Rev. 441, 454 (2014).

[3]   Judicial Conf. Comm. on Codes of Conduct, Fed. Jud. Ctr., Maintaining the Public Trust Ethics for Federal Judicial Law Clerks 1 (2019), *available at* https://cafc.uscourts. gov/wp-content/uploads/HR/Forms/Maintaining-the-Public-Trust_2019-Revised-Fourth-Edition.pdf.

It is important for you to know and understand these rules, as failure to follow them can have dire consequences—both to your clerkship and your legal career. Let me give you an example. A young lawyer working in a clerk-like position lost her job and was sanctioned by the Kansas State Bar for live-tweeting during working hours about a disciplinary case that the Kansas Supreme Court was hearing.[4] She worked for a state intermediate appellate judge, but in the same building as the Kansas Supreme Court.[5] Her tweets did not directly mention her position at the court, but they very clearly gave her view on the matter.[6] When the press found out about her tweets and contacted the court, she was promptly instructed to stop tweeting, placed on leave, escorted out of the building, and fired.[7] She remained unemployed for seven months and was ultimately sanctioned by the state bar.[8] Not a great way to start a legal career!

To give you a taste of the ethical responsibilities clerks face, let me outline the requirements for federal clerks, which are located in the Code of Conduct for Judicial Employees.[9] The Judicial Conference Committee on the Codes of Conduct has created a guide to help federal clerks understand the ethical rules that govern their behavior.[10] The guide divides the ethical responsibilities into the 6 Cs.[11] I will briefly discuss each C.

---

[4]   The full story is recounted in an article by former Texas Appellate Justice John G. Browning. John G. Browning, *It's 3 A.M.: Do You Know What Your Staff Just Posted? Social Media Ethics Pitfalls for Appellate Lawyers and Judges*, 22 J. APP. PRAC. & PROC. 49, 60-61 (2022).

[5]   *Id.*

[6]   *Id.* at 61.

[7]   *Id.* at 61-62.

[8]   *Id.* at 62-64.

[9]   JUDICIAL CONF. COMM. ON CODES OF CONDUCT, *supra* note 3, at 1.

[10]   *Id.* at 2.

[11]   The guide says there are 5 Cs, but I count 6 Cs in the table of contents. I may not be great at math, but I have a toddler, so I can count to six.

Confidentiality

You owe your judge and the court a duty of confidentiality, which extends past your clerkship.[12] This means that you cannot share non-public information about a case or "the decision-making process used by your judge, chambers, and/or court in a prior, pending, or impending case."[13] You can talk generally about how the court operates and about your job, but you should refrain from talking about specific cases and specific aspects of the decision-making process. You also should not share information that you learn about your judge's personal or professional views.[14] This duty of confidentiality, however, does not prevent you from disclosing abusing or harassing conduct by your judge or others.[15]

One of the most interesting aspects of this duty of confidentiality is that you can't even discuss the decision-making process with other court employees who don't work for your judge without your judge's permission.[16] This means that if your judge is on a panel with Judge Perez, and your best friend from law school is clerking for Judge Perez, you can't approach that friend to talk about the case without first asking your judge.

Conflicts of Interest

You also have a duty to avoid conflicts of interest. Conflicts come in many shapes and colors. One type of conflict can be personal—you have a family member who is a lawyer, party, or witness in case.[17] Other conflicts are financial—perhaps you, your spouse, or your domestic partner own stock in a company before the

---

[12]   *Id.* at 5.
[13]   *Id.*
[14]   *Id.* at 7.
[15]   *Id.*
[16]   *Id.* at 8.
[17]   *Id.* at 10.

court.[18] As you are assigned cases from your judge, be on the lookout for conflicts. This type of vigilance will be useful if you plan on having a career in government or academia, where you are often required to file conflict of interest statements.[19]

Conduct

This one is simple—follow the advice of my four-year-old and "be nice." The official Canon directs you to "be patient, dignified, respectful, and courteous to all persons with whom the judicial employee deals in an official capacity, including other employees and the general public,"[20] but if you can't memorize all of that, "be nice" and "don't harass people" works great too. *But,* please report harassment if you experience it, even if it is from your judge. This, sadly, has been a problem in the past, but the federal court system has made great strides in improving reporting systems and awareness of the problem.[21]

Caution

The fourth C is Caution, meaning you need to act with caution when it comes to political and online activities. Regarding political activities, you can vote, but you can't actively campaign, display campaign materials, or give money to campaigns.[22] I have a friend who clerks for a state court judge and under their state rules they are not even allowed to "like" on social media a political page or candidate. This can be a tough restriction if you were a political animal in college or law school. However, rather than view it as a

---

[18] *Id.*

[19] In fact, I have an email in my inbox reminding me that my annual conflict of interest form is due.

[20] *Id.* at 14.

[21] *Id.* at 15.

[22] *Id.*

negative, think of all you will gain with this year or two off from politics:

(1)   Fewer never-ending social media debates;

(2)   More time for other activities that aren't campaigning or arguing about politics on social media;

(3)   More money; and

(4)   Overall less stress in your life.

Concerning social media activity, my advice is to limit your posting to safe topics like (1) your kids or pets; (2) your travel and food; (3) what you are currently streaming; (4) your non-political hobbies; and (5) your favorite sports teams. Remember that, like diamonds, the internet is forever. As a lawyer you should always be careful about what you post on social media. You never know where your career will take you, and you don't want an embarrassing post from your younger years to haunt you at a confirmation hearing. Finally, you should see if your specific judge or court has a social media policy that you are required to follow as a clerk.

Community Activities

As a clerk you may need to limit your volunteer activity. You can volunteer for "charitable, religious, cultural, avocational, and recreational activities," but if your activity "relates in any way to the law or the legal system, *consult with your judge before* engaging in that activity."[23] Be careful about fundraising for groups and be sure to check with your judge before publishing legal scholarship.

---

[23]   *Id.* at 21-22.

Career

This last one is a very important. Unless you want to be a career clerk (a great job), you will need to find a job at some point during your clerkship. That search can create conflicts. Keep your judge informed on your search and check with the ethics officers at the court about what types of signing benefits you can accept from a law firm. Under the federal system you can accept relocation fees during your clerkship, but not general signing bonuses.[24]

Summing It up

I know that this is a lot to keep straight. Let me make it simple by giving you a few tips.

- Pay attention to any ethical training you receive when you start your clerkship.

- If you don't receive training be proactive and ask your judge for their guidelines or any court guidelines.

- When in doubt ask. Ask your judge or ask the ethics officer for the court. You can even call the state bar ethics hotline for advice!

Giving Back to Your Law School Community

Both during and after your clerkship please make a conscious effort to give back to your law school community. You can do this in several ways.

First, be willing to speak to current and former students about clerking. Offer to appear on clerkship panels organized by the career services office. Allow that office to share your contact information with other students who want to clerk for your judge.

---

[24] *Id.* at 25-26.

In essence, be a resource to future clerks! This is especially true if you come from an underrepresented group. According to a report by the National Association for Law Placement (NALP), African American and Hispanic men remain the "most under-represented [demographic group] relative to their share of the [graduating] class."[25]

Overall, the diversity numbers aren't great, and the courts recognize that it is a problem. As Bankruptcy Judge Frank J. Bailey noted, "Exposing students to the law early on through outreach, internships, and collaboration with bar associations and pipeline organizations is key to building a more diverse Judiciary and diverse group of legal professionals."[26]

Second, give back to your law school community by judging skills or other competitions. If you are a trial court clerk, volunteer to help with trial competitions. If you are an appellate clerk, judge the intramural moot court competition at your alma mater. Professors are *always* looking for help. Trust me. If you can't find a professor who needs help, just email me. I am always looking for judges.

Finally, see if you can find a way to bring your judge to campus for events. Contact the legal writing professors, skills professors, student groups, the dean's office, or the career services office. I am sure that there is someone on campus who would love to have your judge guest lecture, judge a competition, speak to students, or just have lunch with students. If you can't find anyone, again, just email me. I would love to welcome your judge to our campus!

---

[25] *A Demographic Profile of Judicial Clerks—2006 to 2016*, NALP BULLETIN (Oct. 2017), *available at* https://www.nalp.org/1017research.

[26] *Judge Focus on Diversity in Clerkship, Internship Hiring*, UNITED STATES COURTS (Apr. 29, 2021), https://www.uscourts.gov/news/2021/04/29/judges-focus-diversity-clerkship-internship-hiring.

The Benefit of Stacking Clerkships

I now only hire people who have had a prior clerkship; I have found that a person who wants to clerk for a second year is almost certain to be one who loves the law, loves thinking about the law, and loves writing and the analytic process.

~Judge Andre Davis[27]

When I graduated from law school, it was common for students who graduated from top law schools to move directly from graduation into federal appellate clerkships. While that still happens—you read the statistics earlier in the book—it is becoming more common for federal appellate judges to prefer candidates who have either prior legal work experience or a prior clerkship.

This "stacking" of clerkships provides a unique opportunity for students from lower ranked schools or with lower grades to move from a less prestigious clerkship to a more prestigious clerkship. It also provides an opportunity to see how different types of courts (trial/appellate or state/federal) operate. And, it broadens your network of former clerks and judges.

I frequently encourage my students to stack clerkships, and I have seen students go from the state supreme court to the federal district court, the federal district court to the federal appellate court, and the state intermediate appellate court to the federal district court. I have even seen students stack clerkships within the same court.

As a personal note, I wish that I had experienced a trial-level clerkship before my appellate clerkship. It would have helped me to

---

27   JUDICIAL CLERKSHIP FORUM: A CONVERSATION WITH 12 JUDGES, AMERICAN BAR ASSOCIATION JUDICIAL DIVISION LAWYERS CONFERENCE 5 (2015).

better understand the appellate process if I knew more about the life cycle of a trial.

The Career Clerk

I will end this Short & Happy guide with one more piece of career advice. If you love clerking, consider finding a spot as a career clerk. While there are some downsides to being a career clerk—most noticeably the ethical restrictions discussed above—there are many benefits, including a flexible schedule that is great if you have young kids. The pay can also be quite good over time. I have several friends who are career clerks, and they love their jobs! If the judges in your jurisdiction don't hire career clerks, see if there are staff attorney positions that resemble career clerk spots. The staff attorneys for the Arizona intermediate appellate courts do similar work to career clerks.

Short & Happy!

- Enjoy your clerkship year! Meet new people and explore a new place.

- Be mindful of your ethical limitations as a clerk. Some of these duties follow you after your clerkship ends.

- Consider "stacking" clerkships.

List of Acronyms and Terminology

1L: First year law student

2L: Second year law student

3L: Third year law student

ABA: American Bar Association

ACS: American Constitution Society

ALJ: Administrative law judges

Biglaw: A term used to refer to large firms that generally employ over 500 attorneys.

CAAF: Court of the Appeals for the Armed Forces

Career clerk: A person who works as a permanent law clerk for the same judge.

CLE: Continuing legal education (also known as mandatory or minimum continuing legal education)

CRF: Courts of Indian Offenses

DEA: Drug Enforcement Administration

DOJ: Department of Justice

DOL: Department of Labor

EFTA: European Free Trade Agreement Court

EOIR: Executive Office for Immigration Review

EPA: Environmental Protection Agency

EU: European Union

Exploding offer: A clerkship offer from a judge that you must accept on the spot.

FBA: Federal Bar Association

"Feeder" judges: Judges whose law clerks are frequently selected to clerk for justices of the Supreme Court. Feeder judges typically sit on the federal appellate bench.

FERC: Federal Energy Regulatory Commission

FJC: Federal Judicial Center

IRS: Internal Revenue Service

JA: Judicial assistant

J.D.: Juris Doctor

Judicial clerkship: A full-time position where a law school graduate works for a judge and completes a variety of tasks delegated by that judge.

LLM: Master of Laws (a graduate qualification in the field of law)

NALP: National Association for Law Placement

OSCAR: Online Systems for Clerkship Applications and Review

SCOTUS: Supreme Court of the United States

Staff attorney: A person who works for the court system handling cases. This person usually works for the clerk of the court or a staff attorney office, not a particular judge.

Term clerkship: A clerkship set for a certain length of time—typically one or two years.